BREWING UP A DAMN GOOD STORY

"YOUNGEST BREWERY OWNERS IN THE WORLD, THE OLDEST BREWERY IN THE MIDWEST AND A WHOLE LOT MORE!"

Lead Writing Team: Manjit, Moni and Ravinder Minhas

Research, Manuscript Review, and Graphic Design (Listed Alphabetically) :

Neeraj Arvikar, Prachi Arvikar, Donna Bahler, Luis Berumen, Allison Cartwright, Michael Connolly,

John Dutcher, Matt Figi, Tami Hoesly, Kathy J. Jones, Cristian Jurcut,

Kris Kalav, Jill Muehrcke, Gary Olson, Cathy Sennett, Mary Soddy and Dick Tschanz.

Photographs and Images Courtesy of (Listed Alphabetically) :

Dave Dukelow, Tami Hoesly, Margaret Pickett (nee Huber),

Noreen Rueckert (Green County Tourism), Mary Soddy (Creative Photography) and Don Storn.

All rights reserved.
Written permission must be secured to use or reproduce any part of this book,
except for brief quotations in critical reviews or articles.
Library of Congress Control Number: 2008 906 235
ISBN : 978-0-9817440-2-5

Published by: **Mountain Crest Publishing SRL LLC**
1315, 14th Avenue, Monroe, Wisconsin 53566 USA
E-mail: 2393772@gmail.com
Printed in Menomonee Falls, Wisconsin, U.S.A. by Inland Graphics.

Dedicated to the most caring, kind and generous lady we have in our lives: our mom - Rani Minhas!

Craft Up Your Life! Cheers!

It gives us great pleasure to note that beer is North America's drink of choice. Beer sales make up more than 50% of all alcoholic drinks sold in the US and Canada.

We are also happy to see that beer has not been subjected to "snobbish appeal" by its "connoisseurs". Unlike wine, no special knowledge is required to enjoy good beer. Can you imagine Homer Simpson drinking Duff wine? You do not have to live a life of the idle rich or get a small mortgage to buy top notch craft beer. You also don't need to get a specialized temperature and humidity controlled beer room or talk like a wine snob or cork dork. Simply put, craft beer is an affordable luxury for everyone.

We are proud to note that craft beers have been growing at a rate of about 15% per year for several years now. In comparison, the mass produced factory beer sales have been declining. This shows Americans as well as our fellow Canadians are becoming appreciative of the quality and diverse taste craft beers have to offer. At Minhas Craft Brewery, we currently make pilsner, bock, farmhouse ale, amber ale, dark lager, ice lager, American and Canadian lagers and pale ale - all made with the finest natural ingredients from around the world. We brew in small batches with our secret recipes created by our brewmasters over the last century and a half. Our beers are all natural and do not contain any preservatives or other unnecessary additives that packaged foods tend to have. What goes in your tummy should matter to you! And what goes in your beer should also matter to you!

You must have tried the mass produced beers that taste like they came from the same tank. Beer does not have to be a commodity in your life. Why not craft up your life and try a few of our craft brews? Try craft beers with a variety of foods. Pairing foods and beers is a fun way to discover a new passion in life. Invite over a few of your friends, bring some fresh foods and pick up a Sampler Pack of our craft beers and discover a new way to enjoy an evening.

Minhas Craft Brewery is a small, independent and traditional 100% family-owned craft brewery. We are a brother-sister team in our 20s that own the Minhas Craft Brewery, making us the youngest brewery owners in the world. Established on the same location in 1845, ours is the oldest brewery in the Midwest, second oldest in the USA and 14th largest in the country. This book tells the story of the Monroe Brewery, its past and present owners and the brews it makes. It also elucidates and demystifies the secrets of the remarkable success we have had. We hope that you will enjoy reading and sharing this book with your friends.

Cheers!

- Ravinder and Manjit Minhas

1. **Monroe, Land of Beer and Cheese** 10

All about the quaint town with a feel of Europe in which the Minhas Craft Brewery is located, and where many of us live, work and raise our families.

2. **Craft Brews That Make You Say "Cheers!"** 22

Details of our flagship brews - Lazy Mutt Farmhouse Ale, Swiss Amber Ale, 1845 PILS and the Fighting Billy Bock.

3. **Minhas School of Beer Business Success** 42

Insight into what makes Ravinder and Manjit Minhas successful in an industry that is known for cutthroat and aggressive competitors.

4. **Owners Present & Past and Their Homegrown Brands** 51

Details of the community leaders and prominent business people who have owned the Brewery over the last 163 years.

5. **Miserable Failure of a "Noble Experiment"** 70

Story of the National Prohibition of Alcohol in the USA and 13 years of legislated hell!

6. **Rescue of Heritage Brands from Now Defunct Breweries** 78

Portrait of the four breweries that were shutdown and thanks to the Monroe Brewery, a number of their heritage brands, such as Augsburger, Berghoff & Rhinelander, were rescued.

7.	**Ad Persuasion**	92	**Index** 106

Examples of advertising, marketing and media strategies as well as tactics utilized over the years.

8. Sweet Libations and New Age Drinks 101

Libations to satisfy your sweet tooth – old fashioned sodas, flavored malt beverages (FMBs) and energy drinks.

PREFACE

In 1867 there were 3,700 breweries in the US, in 1920 there were still over 1,400 in operation; and by 1983 there were only about 80 breweries left. Even with the welcome addition of micro and craft breweries across the country in recent years, there are just a few hundred breweries across the USA and Canada. Despite the popularity of national brands produced by the mega-breweries and supported by their huge advertising budgets, the long held tradition of hundreds of local brands and craft brews continues to prevail. Through this book, we arc presenting to you the amazing story of one of the very few remaining (and still thriving!) breweries in the heartland of America. We are reminded of what Confucius said a long time ago:

> *Choose a job that you love, and you will never have to work a day in your life*
>
> - Confucius

Nothing of any great consequence can be achieved without teamwork, and hard work from a lot of people. We, the writing team of this book, would like to take this opportunity to thank you the reader of this book. We sincerely hope that you will enjoy reading this book as much as we enjoyed putting it together.

Monroe, Land of Beer and Cheese

What makes the City of Monroe special? No, Marilyn Monroe was not born here and from all accounts, she never visited the City of Monroe either. However, the City of Monroe is a quaint and beautiful place. It is like a little Switzerland. The historic Green County Courthouse and the square around it, with its variety of shops, delis, cafes and bars makes it a great gathering place for events and festivals. The Square also has "Baumgartner's", the oldest cheese store in Wisconsin, in the state that is "America's Dairyland". Last (and not least), its quaint downtown is the location of the oldest brewery in the Midwest producing world class craft beers.

Did we pique your interest? Please read on about this great city. We hope you will find it entertaining and informative.

History of Breweries and Prohibition

At the middle of the 19th century, almost every community in the United States had its own brewery and most of them were started by German immigrants. Monroe's brewery was established in 1845 by a Mr. Bissinger. In 1920, when prohibition of alcohol was brought in by the Eighteenth Amendment to the United States Constitution there were 97 breweries in Wisconsin. Starting January 16, 1920, federal prohibition agents (police) were given the task of criminally charging people or companies that manufactured, sold or served alcohol. Prohibition, which lasted 13 years, caused most of the breweries in United States to shut down. The Blumer Brewery (the name of the brewery in Monroe at the time) and a few others survived by making sodas (Minhas Craft Brewery still makes Blumer sodas!), "near beer", (non-alcoholic beer) and ice cream. The Monroe Brewery also dabbled in other businesses such as selling tractors, silo filters and road building machinery for the J. I. Case Threshing Machine Company of Racine, Wisconsin. The end of prohibition in 1933 pumped life back into the brewing business and this continued through the 1950s. The second half of the 20th century brought the final blow to local breweries that were still making a diversified selection of tasty beers for Americans. A handful of mega-breweries put out a few similar tasting brews and were backed by multi-million dollar marketing campaigns. The local breweries that still existed were stamped out. It is a testament to the indomitable spirit of the people of Monroe that not only did its brewery survive - it actually thrived! There is no other community in the United States as small as Monroe (and many times its population!) that has a world class brewery like the Minhas Craft Brewery. It is comforting to see that the revival of craft brewed quality beers in America is taking place and Minhas Craft Brewery is at

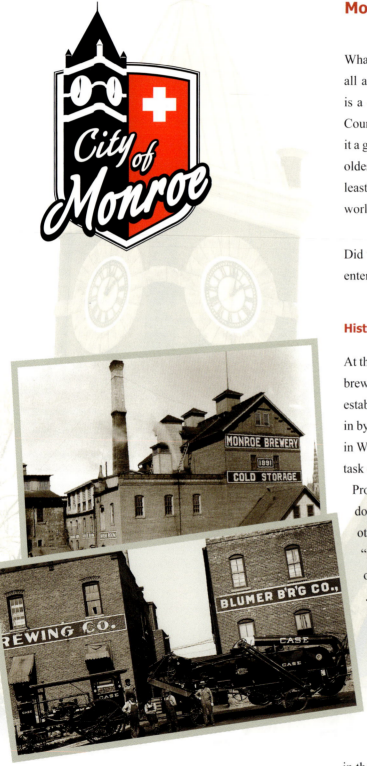

The Brewery in Monroe as it looked in the early 1900s.

the forefront of this revolution. Over the last 163 years, the brewery in Monroe has been owned by the most prominent residents of the city of Monroe of Swiss and German origin - the Martys, the Hubers, the Heftys and the Blumers. This Brewery has made the City of Monroe and Green County better known in every state in the United States as well as many countries in the world such as Canada, Japan, Panama, Ecuador, Brazil, Great Britain, Paraguay, Argentina and Russia.

Location of Monroe

Monroe (population 10,000+) is the largest city in Green County (population 30,000+) which is located in south-central Wisconsin on the Illinois-Wisconsin border. It is located about 45 miles south of Madison, 145 miles west of Chicago and about 100 miles southwest of Milwaukee.

History of Monroe

While neighboring towns and cities have auto plants, glass plants, and many other factories and industries, somehow Monroe has avoided the mega-factories. Instead, as the "Swiss Cheese Capital of the World", Green County has the largest number of master cheesemakers in America. Monroe is also the home of The Swiss Colony, one of the largest mail order businesses in North America with 7,000 of employees shipping millions of packages every year. Monroe has many varieties of dairy cattle, including the spotted cows and the gentle looking Brown Swiss Cows. This area is inhabited with friendly and hardworking people of German (41%), Swiss (24%), Norwegian (15%), Irish (11%) and English (9%) ancestry.

Gentle looking Brown Swiss Cows dot the Green County countryside, surrounding Monroe.

Brewing Up a Damn Good Story

Green County Courthouse, Circa 1891.

Monroe Beginnings

Mr. Paine built the first house in Monroe in 1835. Jarvis Rattan who built the second house was soon followed by Jacob Lybrand who opened a store. Next came a tavern, which was the main social gathering place in those days as the houses were quite small. The first school opened in 1837.

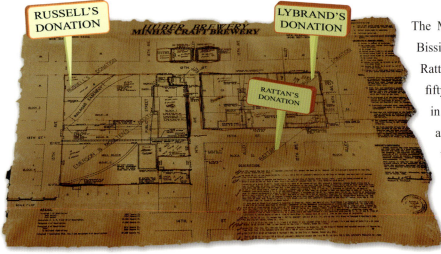

The Monroe Brewery was established in 1845 in downtown Monroe by Mr. Bissinger. Interestingly, the brewery title survey maps show land donations by Rattan and Lybrand. By 1856, a boom of sorts was taking place in Monroe with fifty new buildings under construction. Monroe was incorporated as a village in April 1858 and became a city in 1882. All the initial buildings in Monroe are long gone. Fire destroyed portions of the Brewery on December 27, 1875 with a loss of $8,000 - a princely sum at that time. During the last 163 years, the brewery in Monroe has remained in operation at its original site. During this time, buildings and equipment have been constantly upgraded with the latest technology. The Brewery in Monroe is by far the oldest employer in town and one of the oldest in the state of Wisconsin.

Green County Courthouse.

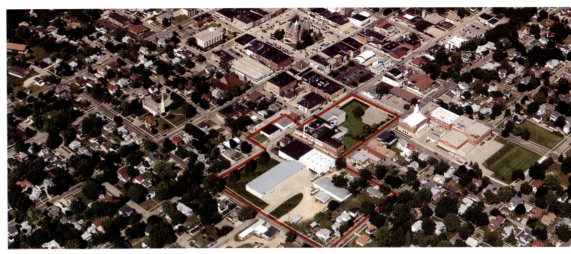
Aerial Photograph of the Brewery with the Courthouse in the background.

The famous Green County Courthouse, built in 1891, remains the focal point of the town square and is listed on the National Register of Historic Places.

The first Cheese Days celebration was held in 1914. At the first Cheese Days, 3,000 cheese sandwiches were prepared by volunteers in the garage of the Brewery (now Minhas Craft Brewery). Cheese Days celebrations are still held every two years (on even years) and attract over 150,000 people - fifteen times the population of Monroe.

Cheese Days 2006.

The above picture was taken in the early 1970s from the Courthouse looking southwest. It shows the brewery in the background. To the Brewery's right is the Jailhouse Tap and the Cheese Factory which with age became structurally unsound and was leveled in 1999. However, its basement was retained to store brewery equipment. This underground "parts room" was finally removed to accommodate the brewery's 50,000 square foot warehouse addition in 2008.

The Turner Hall of Monroe, originally built in 1868, was destroyed by fire in 1936, but was re-opened with a new building on the same site in 1938. A non-profit Swiss heritage and community center, it is listed on the National and State Registers of Historic Places, Turner Hall is the only Turner (gymnast) Hall of Swiss origin left in the United States.

The Turner Hall.

Beers on tap at the Turner Hall.

14 | Monroe, Land of Beer and Cheese

In addition to offering a wide array of Swiss heritage programming throughout the year, Turner Hall houses the Rathskeller Restaurant, which serves excellent Swiss and American cuisine. It has had a historic association with its close neighbor, the Minhas Craft Brewery, and has been serving its beers throughout the decades.

The Monroe Clinic opened in 1936 and is consistently ranked in the Top 100 integrated health care networks in the country. It has 1,100 employees with 75 doctors and surgeons providing

complete medical services. Monroe Clinic has been the primary provider of health services to the staff and management of Minhas Craft Brewery, for many decades. The Monroe Clinic has recently completed a major facility expansion costing $60 million.

Monroe Clinic - a Multi-Specialty Health Care Center and Swiss Colony Head Office, a mail order business.

Throughout the Midwest, one can see a number of roadside signs in front of bars and taverns for many brands produced over the years at the Brewery.

Roadside signs in front of bars and taverns.

Railroad Depot 1922, is now used for the Historic Cheese making Center Museum and Welcome Center.

Cheese Company Row - 1920.

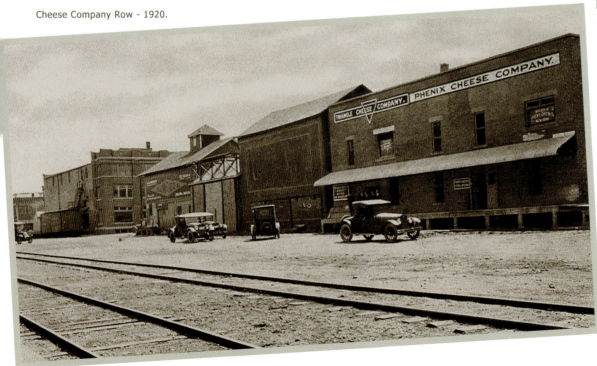

Designed in 1888, the Chicago, Milwaukee and St. Paul Railroad Depot served Monroe for decades. The Depot now serves as the Cheese Making Center and Railroad Museum.

This picture of Monroe taken in 1920 shows Cheese Row on the south side of the Chicago, Milwaukee and St. Paul Tracks.

Monroe is home to many cheese factories. The rail tracks have now been removed and the old rail bed now serves as The Badger State Trail, which is perfect for walking, hiking, cycling and snowmobiling.

The 53 mile long trail connects Freeport, Illinois to the south and to Madison, Wisconsin to the north.

The Cheesiness of Monroe and Green County

Baumgartner's Cheese Store and Tavern, located "on the square" is the oldest cheese store in Wisconsin. It is a great place to purchase beer and aged cheese and to have a meal with friends. Established in 1931, it has not changed much over the years, and that is a good thing. Murals, paintings, a map of the cantons (states) of Switzerland and miscellaneous memorabilia adorn its walls, ceiling, and shelves. Baumgartner's and the Brewery have remained allies over the years; the Brewery frequently sends visitors to savor cheese sandwiches and hometown beer!

Parking meters require 5 cents each hour and a parking violation ticket costs only $5. There are also street names that end with ½. Older people may greet you with "hello" or the Swiss version, "wie gehts!" on the street. The High School teams are called (what else!) "The Cheesemakers". Green County is the home of America's only limburger producing cheese factory still in existence. Businesses such as Ford, GM, Chrysler, and Toyota dealerships as well as McDonalds, Wal-Mart, Shopko, Pick'n Save, Piggly Wiggly, Walgreen and Pizza Hut dot the newer section of Monroe on its west side.

The local newspaper, the Monroe Times still retains the flavor of a small town newspaper. It still lists the people who were unfortunate enough to get vehicle and other legal violations - which hopefully serves as a deterrent. Monroe is the kind of town where a few people still do not bother to lock their house or car. Being a family oriented community, neighbors tend to keep an eye out for each other.

Things To Do when visiting Monroe

If you are in the Monroe area, you can enjoy farm, cheese factory and brewery tours. The "Best Brewery Tour in America" at the Minhas Craft Brewery by itself is worth a trip. There are museums such as the Historic Cheesemaking Center and the Green County Historical Museum. The Rathskeller at Turner Hall of Monroe displays exhibits of local Swiss history and irreplaceable artwork. Minhas Craft Brewery also has museum and gift center. Most of the buildings on and around Monroe's Square are on the National Register of Historic Places. Monroe Arts Center, located in the Old Methodist Church, hosts art shows and performances. Monroe as a popular tourist destination has a lot to offer. There are several bed and breakfast accommodations as well as campgrounds in the area. And don't forget to take home the best beer and cheese anywhere - at Baumgartner's, Alp & Dell and Brennan's and many area cheese factories and stores. Monroe is indeed an enchanting place to visit!

An alphorn trio calls to the cows.

A Day In The Life Of Monroe

> *Monroe, is a quaint little town in southern Wisconsin with a lot of cows, cheese and a beer enjoying problem. Their biannual fair is called Cheese Days, their sports teams are called the Cheesemakers and their passion is world class beer making. I guarantee you that there is no other town in America that can claim such a distinction. Here is to Monroe and its brewers and cheesemakers!*
>
> *- Manjit Minhas*

CHEESE DAYS, A TRADITION SINCE 1914

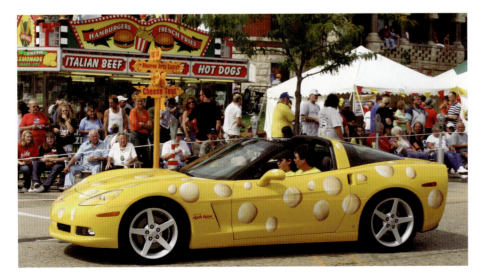 

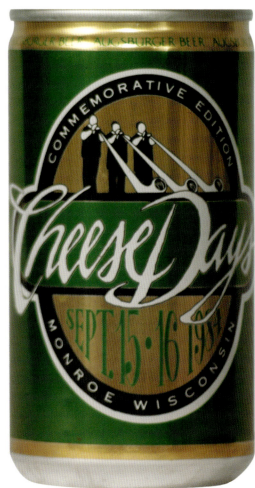

Brewing Up a Damn Good Story 21

Craft Brews That Make You Say "Cheers!"

On October 3, 2006, the brother and sister team of Ravinder and Manjit Minhas (both in their mid 20s) purchased the Brewery in Monroe, Wisconsin. This made them the youngest brewery owners in the world. This was also the beginning of a new era in the storied history of the Brewery. This meant more than $5 million in capital investments, including new buildings, equipment and facilities; a new approach to marketing; a commitment to environmental stewardship and active community involvement, and perhaps most importantly - new beers and brands.

The team at Minhas Craft Brewery felt that they represented the future of the craft beer industry in Canada and the USA. A decision was made to create four new craft beers that represent the vision of the future. A year of research, development and experimentation ensued and four new world class craft beers were produced.

- Lazy Mutt Farmhouse Ale

- Swiss Amber Ale

- Fighting Billy Bock

- 1845 "All Malt" PILS

" A good batch of beer is like a ton of happiness waiting to come out. "

- Manjit Minhas

Lazy Mutt Farmhouse Ale, Man's Best Friend

Background on Farmhouse Ales

The term "farmhouse ales" conjures up romantic images of a refreshing beer brewed on picturesque farms in the Flanders region of Belgium.

Not long ago, hundreds of small independent breweries dotted the Belgian countryside.

In the Flanders region of the Belgian farm country, a farmhouse brewery or a village co-op brewery would brew beer called "saisons" at the beginning of winter in order to quench the thirst of the hard working farmers and the farmhands (called "saisoners") who worked in the fields in the summer. The saisoners consumed an average of five liters a day; therefore, the farmhouse ales were intended to refresh and not to inebriate. This explains the reason that the alcohol content in the farmhouse ales was a moderate 5%, and not the usual higher alcohol percentage many old beer recipes tended to have.

The longer aging time and the bottle conditioning softened the edges, making the farmhouse ales smooth and very easy drinking. The farmers also added "spelt" which is a form of wheat into the mash. The higher protein content contributed to the impression of a fuller mouth feel and body, than the measured gravity. The farmhouse breweries usually grew their own barley and wheat and malted it themselves, always using the finest ingredients available since it was for their own consumption.

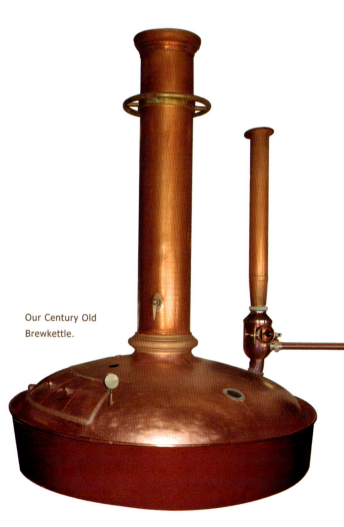

Our Century Old Brewkettle.

> *If we do not like the results,*
> *it is necessary for us to change our inputs and attitudes.*
> *The results will be the same again*
> *if the conditions that brought the undesirable results*
> *are not dramatically changed.*
> *This applies to life as well as in business*
> *- and yes, even in the beer business.*
>
> — *Manjit Minhas*

In Flanders Fields the poppies blow
Between the crosses row on row,
That mark our place; and in the sky
The larks, still bravely singing, fly
Scarce heard amid the guns below.

We are the Dead. Short days ago
We lived, felt dawn, saw sunset glow,
Loved and were loved, and now we lie
In Flanders fields.

Take up our quarrel with the foe:
To you from failing hands we throw
The torch; be yours to hold it high.
If ye break faith with us who die
We shall not sleep, though poppies grow
In Flanders fields.

In Flanders Fields
By: Lieutenant Colonel John McCrae, MD (1872-1918) Canadian Army.

As industrialization grew, a large number of people moved from the rural to urban areas of Belgium. As a result, many small breweries closed. Consolidation squeezed out the small brewer, resulting in very few large breweries controlling the national market.

The market was slowly and deliberately ground down into industrialized blandness with two or three companies making practically identical brews. This story should sound familiar to the students of Canadian and American brewing industry as it closely parallels recent history in North America. For the past few decades, a revolution of sorts is taking place across Belgium. There are now a dozen farmhouse breweries started by young couples determined to revive the lost art of farmhouse ales, inspired by their rich beer culture, and their deep love of beer and brewing.

Most are very small breweries and do not export their products out of their local area. They are located in cute little farm buildings with spacious inner courtyards and café/tasting rooms where visitors can sit down and sample the beers. The beautiful fruit orchards extend in all directions, which make for some great hiking. A number of small travel operators are now offering brewery tours throughout the Belgian countryside.

Lazy Mutt Farmhouse Ale

Lazy Mutt Farmhouse Ale is a tribute by Ravinder and Manjit Minhas to their Canadian heritage and the very famous poem they learned in school "In Flanders Field" composed by John McCrae. It was written in appreciation of the sacrifice of the Canadian soldiers in World War I in the Flanders area of Belgium. It is also a tribute to the beautiful Green County in southern Wisconsin where the Minhas Craft Brewery is located.

Parallel to the growth of the Belgian farmhouse breweries over the last two decades, a micro and craft brewing revolution is also taking place in North America, led by Sam Adams and Sierra Nevada in the USA and by Big Rock Brewery in Canada. The craft brewery segment is growing in North America at an astonishing 15% per year while the rest of the beer sales volume is declining.

Minhas Craft Brewery (MCB) continues this revolution with the introduction of Lazy Mutt Farmhouse Ale. MCB wanted to brew a farmhouse ale that kept its traditional qualities of being aged longer, having greater mouth feel and providing the smooth velvety taste of a bottle conditioned ale. Minhas Craft Brewery believes that a beer is not the exclusive domain of its country of origin. For example, Pilsner got its start from the Pilsen area in Czechoslovakia and yet excellent Pilsners are now made around the world. MCB believes that, in today's small world, styles and techniques of beer belong to everybody. It may sometimes take the enthusiasm of an outsider with a passion to explore things that the originating area may take for granted.

WHAT DOES IT MEAN TO BE MAN'S BEST FRIEND?

It means we're always there when you need us.

We're your wingman, your ice-breaker, your seat-saver, your, well, you get the idea.

It means that on Sunday, when you have two things on your mind: where to sit and what to watch, we'll be right there with you. ENJOY AT WILL.

Tasting Notes

Lazy Mutt is an unfiltered ale, cloudy and pale in color. The off-white foam slowly disappears to reveal a slight citrus aroma. A citrusy palate gives way to a light malty sweetness touched by a hint of corn. Lazy Mutt can be enjoyed with many foods from fresh garden vegetables to hearty meat dishes to fruit compotes. For snacking, it goes great with Swiss, Cheddar, Havarti, Provolone and Muenster cheeses as well as fresh cheese curds.

Lazy Mutt has won a Bronze Medal in the 2008 World Beer Championships Beverage Testing Institute Awards.

Beer Specifications

Style:	Farmhouse Ale
Malt Varieties:	2 row base malt, caramel, Vienna, wheat and flaked barley
Hop Varieties:	Galena and Tettnang
Specific Gravity:	1.01180
Alcohol By Volume (ABV):	5.0%
Alcohol by Weight (ABW):	4.0%
Color:	4.29
pH:	4.21
Calories:	159.42
IBU (International Bitterness Units):	7

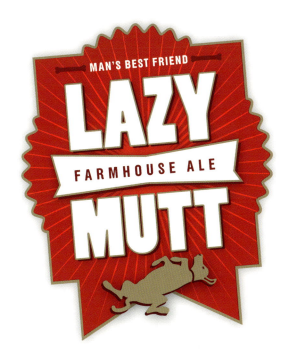

Swiss Amber Ale - Not The Ordinary, The Extraordinary !

Minhas Craft Brewery is located in Monroe, Wisconsin. The City of Monroe is a quaint and a beautiful place. It is like a little Switzerland with its Swiss Heritage buildings and the number of people who still speak the Swiss German language. Set in the beautiful green rolling hills of southern Wisconsin, Green County is dotted with red and white barns, and many varieties of dairy cattle including the gentle looking Brown Swiss. The cow population in Green County actually exceeds people.

Swiss Amber Ale is a dedication to and appreciation of the Swiss culture with its hard working people and the tradition of producing the finest quality products. It is a tribute to the Brewery's Swiss origin owners and workers - past and present.

Tasting Notes

At first glance, this reddish-copper ale looks strong and heavy, but one sip proves that it's smooth as silk. Slight citrus notes greet you while aromatic hops tingle on your tongue. A smooth, clean finish waits at the bottom of the glass. Swiss Amber Ale is made with Brewer's 2-Row Malt, CaraPils Malt, Caramel Malts and domestic hops. The alcohol content is 5.5% by volume.

Beer Specifications

Specific Gravity:	1.00860
Apparent Extract:	2.20
Alcohol By Volume (ABW):	4.38
Alcohol By Volume (ABV):	5.50
Original Extract:	12.30
Color:	17 L
pH:	4.25
IBU (International Bitterness Units)	21

NOT THE ORDINARY. THE EXTRAORDINARY! Monroe, a quaint town located

in the beautiful hills of Southern Wisconsin - also called "Swiss Cheese Capital of the World"

- hosts "CHEESE DAYS" every two years. The friendly, hard working people

put on a grand show, with the town's population exploding by 15 times.

The parade features plenty of majestic Brown Swiss Cows.

Grab a cold one and savor the joy, the peace and the neutrality

the Swiss have given to mankind!

1845 "All Malt" PILS, Mr. Corn and Mr. Rice Do Not Live Here

Heritage and tradition of virtual handcrafting of the finest beers in the world goes back to 1845 at the family-owned Minhas Craft Brewery located in Monroe, Wisconsin.

History of Pils

There are three names used for the same style of beer - Pilsner, Pilsener or Pils. About 50% of all beer sold in the world is the Pils style - although many of them have cheapened the original recipe and therefore compromised its taste.

The history of Pils goes back to 1838 when the brewmasters in Pilsen, Bohemia (the Czech Republic now) rolled 36 barrels of ale out into the street, opened them up, and spilled the beer in the main square of town letting it run into the ditches and finally into the nearby Radbuza River. The brewers had decided that the ale had become undrinkable. Even for breweries of Pilsen with over 800 years of brewing experience, it was not uncommon for beers having to be discarded due to contamination by wild yeasts or bacteria. This incident upset the brewmasters so much that they were determined not to repeat it ever again.

The brewers felt that they needed to change things drastically to avoid this type of disaster. They hired a Bavarian brewmaster Josef Groll. He brought a special yeast to Pilsen and taught them the proper method of lagering beer. They also started using the Noble Saaz hops produced in the area. A new recipe was born. Using light barley that was only partially malted and none of the roasted or smoked barley that the German brewers were using, Groll added generous portions of the fragrant Saaz hops to his brew. On October 5, 1842 he and the other brewers of Pilsen gathered for their first taste of the new beer. They fell in love with the straw colored beer, and the rest, as they say, is history. This style of beer quickly became extremely popular.

Many breweries have changed the Pils recipe to cut costs. Such variations include replacing part of the barley with corn syrup or rice. Rice is cheap and contributes little flavor or aroma to the brew. The result is a beer with less flavor and aroma, making it taste watery when compared to 100% barley pilsners. Many beer connoisseurs feel that if they wanted rice in their drink, they would drink sake and if they wanted the taste of rice and malt together, they would eat Rice Krispies cereal!

The commercially available Pilsner brands on the market are Czech Budvar, Stella Artois, Pilsner Urquell, Heineken, Beck's and Bitburger.

38 DEGREE PARADISE

Chill it to 38° F, sit in your favorite chair and sip away the 38 Degree Paradise. Here is to hoping that you own a fridge dedicated to chilling beer to its perfect temperature! Did you know that 1845 is an ALL MALT beer made in the finest Euro tradition? Mr. Corn and Mr. Rice don't live here! They are not even welcome here. 1845 PILS is our Brewmaster's dream and hopefully, it will also become yours.

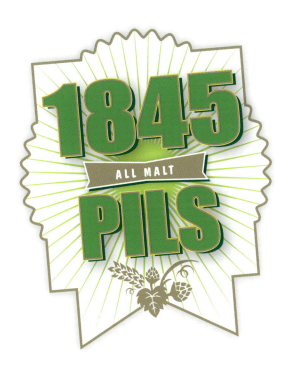

Making of the 1845 "all malt" PILS

The team at the Minhas Craft Brewery came up with a beer made in the old world European tradition as a tribute to the brewery's brewmasters - past and present. It is also a dedication to the heritage and tradition passed on by each successive brewmaster who worked at the Brewery in the past century and a half.

As the mega-brewers work harder to reduce the cost of their beer, they reduce the more expensive malts and increase the use of adjuncts such as rice, corn syrup, dextrose and other cheaper ingredients. This results in a reduction in taste and leaves the discerning craft beer consumer with fewer acceptable choices. A PILS beer is easy drinking as well as it is tastier, less hoppy and has more balanced taste profile. 1845 "all malt" PILS is a perfect choice for that leisurely hot summer day when nothing else seems to matter. The tranquility of life needs to be enjoyed with an affordable luxury.

The sparkling mouth feel of each sip of our 1845 "all malt" PILS confirms the dedication to virtual handcrafting of our craft beers. Every aspect of the brewing process of the family-owned Minhas Craft Brewery translates into the special 1845 PILS that sets it apart from other beers.

Like champagne, the quality of a great PILS can be seen in the density of its bubbles. 1845 PILS produces small, tight bubbles that rise from the bottom of the glass, delivering a slightly spicy aroma and malty taste. This perfect balance of flavors is achieved by procuring the exact blend of malt and hops and fermenting the brew with our proprietary yeast. The signature of 1845 PILS is its finish. The crisp, clean and well-rounded taste leaves just a subtle touch of soft bitter flavor on the back of the palate.

We use 2 row US and Canadian malts and the finest hops to make 1845 PILS. They cost more and have less yield; however, they produce a much cleaner tasting beers. We do not use any adjuncts such as rice or corn, and we do not use any preservatives or additives. It should also be noted that there are almost 100 approved preservatives and additives for beers; however, we do not use any of them. We make it in small 350 barrel batches and then we age 1845 "all malt" PILS 50% longer than others. Yes, it costs us a lot more to make this beer but it is no wonder that the result is a true European quality PILS without compare.

> *Hops are plants, and they're actually part of the same botanical family as hemp. In A.D. 1200, beer-brewing monks first discovered that hops both preserve beer and give it that distinctive, slightly bitter taste.*

- Hops, an important ingredient in making beer

Tasting Notes

A truly classic old-world pilsner beer, 1845 PILS starts out with light malt aromas followed by floral hop scents. A brilliant hop bitterness rolls lightly to the sides of the tongue, refreshed and cleansed with each sip. A perfect accompaniment to any meal, 1845 PILS matches even the most discriminating palate. The alcohol content is 5.5% by volume.

Beer Specifications

Specific Gravity:	1.00700
Apparent Extract:	1.80
Alcohol By Volume (ABW):	4.38
Alcohol By Volume (ABV):	5.50
Original Extract:	11.80
Color:	5 L
pH:	4.25
IBU (International Bitterness Units)	18

> *In 1810, Prince Ludwig of Bavaria married Princess Theresa. Their wedding reception turned into a 16 day beer party, one that was repeated the following year. Soon it became known as "Oktoberfest," giving young blonde girls in billowy blouses a reason to lug around oversized beer steins.*

Fighting Billy Bock

The bock style of beer was invented in the early 14th century in the town of Einbeck in north Germany. Over the years, these beers became very popular.

It is amusing to read what a 16th century historian writes about what he claims are bock beer's medicinal and non-fattening benefits:

"Of all summer beers, the bock beer is the most famed and deserves the preference. Each third grain to this beer is wheat; hence, too, it is of all barley beers the best . . . People do not fatten too much from its use; it is also very useful in fever cases."

Bock beer goes back to the days when monks brewed much of the beverage in Bavaria and needed a heavy, carbohydrate-laden beer to provide sustenance through the weeks of fasting after Lent. Originally, bock beers were brewed in the fall, aged through the winter and celebrated in the spring at traditional Bavarian bock beer festivals. There is no longer any seasonal connection to bock beer.

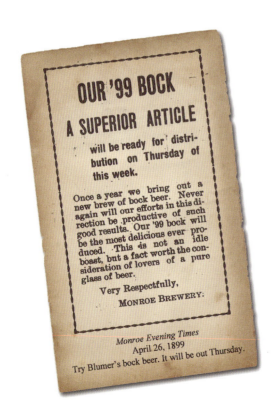

Here is an ad in Monroe's local newspaper the "Monroe Evening Times" dated April 26, 1899. Its readers are being asked to "Try Blumer's Bock Beer. It will be out Thursday"

Our Brewery was one of the first to introduce bock beers in the US during the second half of the 19th century. Bock beers are sustaining, very smooth lagers, and dark in color. Our Brewery released its bock beer every year in celebration of the coming of spring as part of an ancient and mysterious part of the brewing tradition.

It was traditional to launch bock beers as seasonal beers every spring.

Almost every brewery in US followed the lead of our Brewery and produced a bock beer of their own. The onset of Prohibition in 1920 stopped production of all bock (and other) beers across the country. After Prohibition was repealed in 1933, the tradition of spring bock beers dwindled and only a few Breweries still make the bock style of beer. However, our Brewery has continued with pride the tradition of brewing the finest bock beers for over 160 years.

Consumers like its dark, flavorful and yet light in alcohol features (5.5% Alcohol By Volume). Our bock has a pronounced malty aroma and flavor that dominates over the clean, crisp, moderate hop bitterness. It has a relatively low bitterness and a chocolate-like, roast malt, bread-like aroma. "Bock" in German means "goat" and that is why one sees an image of goat on most bock labels. In the old days, bock beers were quite strong and possibly the "kick" they gave, reminded people of the goat as well.

Tasting Notes

Fighting Billy Bock Beer is a rich, flavorful, full-bodied beer reminiscent of traditional German bock beers of the past. As you lift the glass, malty sweet aromas fill your senses with a caramel sweetness. A gentle mix of floral scents greets the palate with a distinct yet delicate hop bitterness. Robust smoothness defines this classic beer. Fighting Billy Bock is made with Brewer's 2-Row Malt, CaraPils Malt, Caramel Malt, Black Malt and domestic hops. The alcohol content is 5.5 % by volume.

> *I believe the two best jobs in the world are teaching kindergarten and being a beer guy. If I ever retire from the beer business (not likely!), you know what I will do for a living!*
>
> *- Ravinder Minhas*

HELP DISPEL THE CURSE

The curse can easily be dispelled by showing a sincere fondness for Billy Bock.

It fights only to maintain its dignity.

What does the "=" sign mean?

It explains the relationship between BOCK and TASTE.

Simply put BOCK = TASTE.

Chill Billy Bock to 45° F (7° C),

call over three of your best buddies and help dispel the curse.

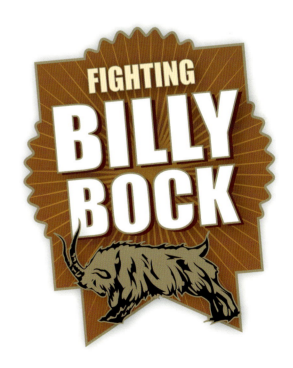

" *In the Middle Ages, a liquid lunch was known as "nunchion," a combination of "noon scheken," or "noon drinking." Along with your beer, you would also enjoy a large chunk of bread, which was called "lunch". Soon, "having a luncheon" would denote having a piece of bread and a pint of beer in the middle of the day.* "

- Luncheon, a popular expression that originated from beer

Beer Specifications

Specific Gravity:	1.01450
Apparent Extract:	3.70
Alcohol By Volume (ABW):	4.38
Alcohol By Volume (ABV):	5.50
Original Extract:	13.75
Color:	35 L
pH:	4.25
IBU (International Bitterness Units)	22

Our bock beers have won numerous awards over the years. This includes a Gold Medal in the 2004 World Beer Championship and "Best American made bock beer" by *Consumer Digest*.

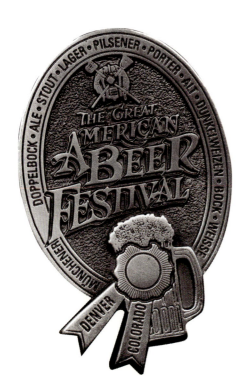

160 Years Of Making Bock

Brewmasters And Creators Of Our Craft Brews

Kris Kalav

Kris Kalav is a brewmaster extraordinaire. He is dedicated to brewing (and drinking!) the finest beer in the nation. He graduated from the University of Illinois, in Chicago with a Bachelor of Science degree.

Since 1995, Kris has created recipes for almost all genres of craft brews for Minhas Craft Brewery. Brews created by Mr. Kalav have won numerous World Beer Gold Medals and Cups. Highly respected in the brewing industry, Kris appears frequently on television news programs and radio talk shows to discuss brewing and beer, along with cheese and food pairings.

Tim Lenahan

Tim Lenahan is a Master Brewer and brewery engineer. Tim has served in senior brewing operations positions at Stroh's Brewery in Detroit, Michigan and Coors Brewery in Golden Colorado. He has been the creative brewing force behind the establishment of seven micro breweries and brewpubs throughout the USA and other countries, including the Breckenridge Brewery (Denver, Colorado), the Tommyknocker Brewery (Idaho Springs, Colorado), Crested Butte Brew Pub (Crested Butte, Colorado) and Snake River Brewery (Jackson Hole, Wyoming). Tim's formulations have garnered a dozen gold medals and other awards since 1991. Tim Lenahan is an instructor and a consultant for the famous Siebel and the World Brewing Technology School.

"The most creative beer culture on the planet is right here in the US. Look at all the great beers coming out of the hundreds of craft and micro breweries in the country."

- Manjit Minhas

Tyler Peters

Tyler Peters has a Bachelor of Science degree from the University of Wisconsin, Madison and has worked as Head Brewer at Lost Coast Brewery in Eureka, California. He interned for 2 years at our brewery, closely working with Kris Kalav, the Brewmaster. Mr. Peters has created several recipes and produced craft beers of almost all types including stouts, wit ale, India pale ale, brown ale and amber ale. Tyler was the lead brewer in the creation of the 1845 "all malt" PILS.

Tribute to our Brewmasters and Medals Won

The brewmaster of a brewery is like a chef in a five star rated fine restaurant who has the masterful ability to transform sustenance into a culinary wonder. A brewmaster does the magical job of choosing from about a dozen malts (2 row, 6 row and specialty malts), various type of hops and yeasts, and converting them into a beer that is perfect every time. It should be noted that a beer recipe, by its very nature, is very complex – a lot more complicated than any other type of wine, spirit or another alcohol. The quality of water, the fermentation temperature and ageing time also provide infinite variations in the final taste of the beer. Some recipes take many months to create and years to perfect. And in a mid size brewery like ours, we do not have an army of brewmasters, each concentrating on a small area. Our brewmaster has to know the operation from the front door to the back, and down the street and around the corner.

"UNION MADE" LOGO ON EACH CAN AND BOTTLE
In 2007, we voluntarily put a UNION MADE label
on each of our cans and bottles.
This was our way of demonstrating support
for our brewery workers who are the best in the business.
It also acknowledges the great relationship
we have with the
International Brotherhood of Teamsters
- Union Local 744.

> *Life is too short to drink cheap beer.*
> *But it is also a crime to drink an over priced beer.*
> *Great tasting beer at an affordable price – now we are talking!*

- Ravinder Minhas

> *Adding yeast to beer mix is a tricky procedure.*
> *If the mix is too cold, the yeast won't have enough*
> *heat to grow. Too hot, and the yeast will burn up and die.*
> *Before brewers had fancy tools like thermometers,*
> *they had to rely on their own thumb to gauge the temperature.*
> *If the mix felt right, the yeast went in.*
> *This became known as the "rule of thumb".*

- *Rule of thumb, a popular expression that originated from beer*

Over the last 163 years, our Brewery in Monroe has been blessed with some of the most innovative brewmasters in the industry. Here is a tribute to all of them - many of whose names we can not re-trace. Thanks to their hard work, talent and experience, we have a vault full of recipes that we use to produce great quality beers everyday. It is of great pride and comfort to us that in our vault we have several more tried and true recipes that we do not produce at this time (including the original Augsburger recipe), but having these recipes allows us to re-introduce these beers and new ones at any time in the future. This helps ensure that the Brewery will be around for another 163 years! Here is a partial list of our brewmasters since the inception of the Brewery in Monroe:

1845 - 1918 : The Brewery Owners

1918 - 38 : Adam Blumer Jr., Mr. Denkoff, Mr. Bruetting, Mr. Haberstumpf

1939 - 41 : Roland Gunther

1942 - 45 : George L. Schwarz

1945 : John Bauer

1946 : Edward Rath

1949 - 66 : Alois Pels

1964 - 67 : Ted Eisch

1970s - 85 & 1989 - 2002 : Hans Kestler

1973 - 92 : Dave Radzanowski

1996 to Now : Kris Kalav

38 | Craft Brews That Make You Say "Cheers!"

Awards and Medals Won by the Brewery

Our brewery has a great reputation of making World Class Beers thanks to the contributions of our past and present brewmasters.

Here is a partial list of awards and medals the Brewery has won:

- 3 Gold, 7 Silver and 3 Bronze medals at the *World Beer Cup Championships*.

- 2 Silver and 3 Bronze medals at the *Great American Beer Festival*.

- 2 Gold, 16 Silver and 2 Bronze medals at *The Beverage Testing Institute*.

In addition, our brews have won numerous accolades such as:

- "Top beer in the USA" in *The Connoisseur Guide to Beer*.

- "First Place" in the *New York Times* Taste Test.

Was the Brewery Founded in 1845 Or 1848?

For many years, the Brewery had been using the slogan "Born with the State" as Wisconsin became a state in 1848. In the 1990s, based on local recorded history, it was discovered and proved, without a doubt, that the Brewery was founded on the same location in 1845.

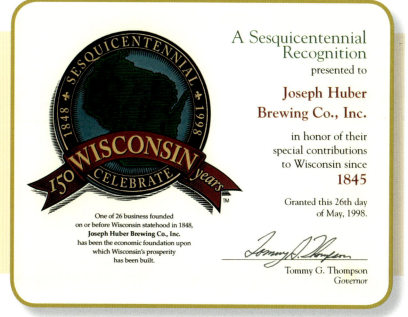

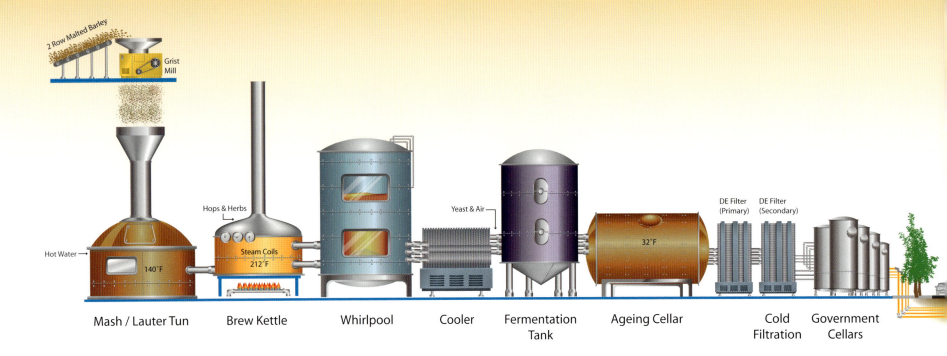

How Do We Brew Damn Good Beer?

It is the precise recipe and timing of the brew that gives one beer taste different from another - even though the main ingredients of beer making have remained the same over the centuries. Damn Good Beer starts with the choicest natural ingredients: barley malt from the fertile prairies of Western Canada and the USA, hops from the American Pacific Northwest of the USA, B.C. of Canada and from Europe and finally, pure pristine water. These ingredients are craft brewed in small batches of 200 to 350 barrels to ensure its quality and attention to detail.

Grist Mill

The malted barley is crushed and ground in the Grist Mill, which cracks open their husks and exposes the starches within. After milling, it is gravity fed into the Mash/Lauter Tun on the floor below.

Mash/Lauter Tun

The crushed grain is steeped in hot (but not boiling) water usually at 140°F - just as you "brew" tea by steeping in hot water. The resulting porridge-like mixture is known as "mash". The malt is added to heated, purified water through a carefully controlled time and temperature process to make the mash. The malt enzymes break down the starch to sugar, flavors from grains are absorbed and the sweet liquid is filtered out of the mash, using the perforated "false" bottom that lets liquid fall through, but not grain husks. It is also equipped with rotating arms that agitate the mash. A technique called "sparging" is also used where hot water is sprayed over the mixture to ensure that every bit of sugar is extracted from the grain. The liquid called "wort" is sent out to the Brew Kettle and the spent grain rich in nutrients is delivered to the dairy farmers in the area for feeding their cows.

Brew Kettle

The wort is boiled in the Brew Kettle for more than an hour usually at more than 212°F. We now add the hops, blossoms of a climbing vine, that impart herbal aromas and flavors to the beer and add "bitterness" and "the distinct spiciness of the beer" to balance the wort's malty sweetness. Boiling helps transfer the characteristics of the hops into the wort. Hops also provide natural components that protect the finished brew against spoilage. We also add herbs and other ingredients to the Brew Kettle - depending on the recipe. The Brew Kettle has steam coils on the inside, designed to create a rolling boil. The boiling process darkens the color and caramelizes the wort to give caramel, toffee and liquorice notes.

Whirlpool

The hopped wort is now pumped to the Whirlpool at a tangent to start swirling action inside. The centrifugal force generated causes hop residue and other unwanted material (like proteins and sneaky husks) to settle towards the center of the vessel's bottom. This results in clear wort.

Cooler

The hopped and clarified wort needs to be cooled now as the yeast we add in the fermentation tanks gets uncomfortable if the wort is too hot. Yeast is just like us - it needs nutrients, air and perfect temperature to do its magic. The wort is now cooled in a Plate and Frame Heat Exchanger, usually to about 60°F for ales or to 50°F for lagers. It should be pointed out that throughout the beer making process, we use energy and water conservation procedures to be kind to the planet we inhabit.

Fermentation Tanks

The wort is now sent to the Fermentation Tanks - we have 12 of these tanks with a capacity of 7,000 barrels. Our proprietary yeast and air are injected inline as the liquid enters the Fermentation Tanks. Yeast is a single-cell critter found in many varieties, from the wild stuff in apple orchards to the packaged kind loved by bread makers. But it all works in the same way. A yeast cell "eats" a molecule of sugar and

How we make Damn Good Beer?

14th Avenue — Canning, Bottling or Kegging — Warehouse & Distribution Center — Shipping & Transportation

gives off, as by-products, alcohol and carbon dioxide (fizz!). The yeast takes the sugary products in the wort and converts them into alcohol and carbon dioxide. Beer yeasts basically come in two types. "Ale Yeast" works at warm temperatures (60°-70°F) and usually produces "fruity" flavor compounds as by-products of fermentation. "Lager Yeast" prefers a cooler environment (50°-60°F) and works more slowly, yielding fewer distinct flavors. The fermentation process takes about a week. The beer at the end of fermentation, called "Green Beer", would be recognizable to anyone as beer - it has bubbles from the carbon dioxide and it has alcohol. The taste is harsh, however, and the beer requires cold aging to allow the flavors to round out and mature. The spent yeast drops off the bottom and is sold to companies for recycling and for use in other industries.

Ageing Cellars

The filtered Green Beer is sent to one of the Ageing Cellars. We have 30 Ageing Tanks with a capacity of 32,000 barrels. We need all of this ageing capacity for the extra ageing we do for our beers. The beer is cooled to 32°F and aged to round out and stabilize the flavors for a minimum of two weeks - usually more depending on the recipe. At the end of ageing period, the beer is almost ready to drink.

DE Filter (Primary)

The Green Beer is now filtered in a DE Filter (Diatomaceous Earth Filter).

DE Filter (Secondary)

The beer is given a final fine cold filtration to ensure that our beer is at the peak of perfection.

Government Cellars

The alcohol in the beer is adjusted to the exact alcohol per volume as per the recipe by adding pure water. It now is stored in one of the Government Cellars - we have 12 of these glass-lined stainless steel tanks with a capacity of 6,000 barrels.

Canning, Bottling Or Kegging

We now pump the beer through a tunnel under the 14th Avenue (yes, one street in Monroe does have beer running underneath it!), pasteurize it and package it in our Bottlehouse "across the street". We package our beers in cans (12 oz., 16 oz., 24 oz. or 5 Liter mini Kegs), in bottles (12 oz. or 40 oz.) or put them in Kegs (1/4 barrel or ½ barrel). The beer is than palletized and placed in our Warehouse and Distribution Center for shipping.

Warehousing and Distribution Center

We have over 50,000 Square Foot of space to store and ship all the different brands and brews of damn good beers we make.

Shipping and Distribution

Our beers are shipped by trucks within USA, by train to markets in Canada and by sea vessels to Japan and other countries.

…..AND THAT IS HOW WE BREW DAMN GOOD BEER!

Minhas School of Beer Business Success

Ravinder and Manjit Minhas are sought after guest speakers at many conventions, conferences and universities. The story of success of the Minhas Craft Brewery and its brands has been extensively featured in the media. The most common question asked by the media and other people is: "What is the secret of your success?" As usual, the answer is neither simple nor mystical. In this Chapter, Ravinder and Manjit Minhas give out their secrets in their own words. We believe these secrets are equally applicable to other businesses and life in general:

Tips for Success

Always Dress Well

We started in the business when we were very young. We noticed that people did not take us seriously if we went out dressed in jeans. We started dressing in the best business suits money can buy. That made all the difference in the world. Other people thought we were older than we really were and that really helped. Now, we are often the best dressed people in the meetings we attend, and we find that this always works in our favor.

There is No Substitute for Hard Work

You have heard "Work Smart Not Hard". This might be true but we find that you simply can not work smart without working hard. As the leader of any organization, one has to be the hardest working member of the team. Yes, it is important to be smart, to delegate and to plan; however, there is simply no substitute for hard work.

Trust and Be Trusted

This sounds old fashioned but we find that when we trust others, they seem to trust us in return. And surprisingly, our trust has rarely been betrayed. We came close to losing a lot of money once but we find that when we use our instincts to judge people and companies and then trust others, we succeed. We frequently transfer funds and send products to customers and suppliers in Canada, the USA, Japan, and other countries - primarily based on trust. We find that we grow and prosper as a result.

Do Not Sleep with an Elephant

"Remain fiercely independent. Do not sleep with an elephant. If the elephant takes a turn, it will hurt you". It has been proposed to us a few times that we produce or sell almost exclusively to a multi-national company. It sounds great but upon closer examination, we have found out that the risks outweigh the rewards. Also, we are always concerned that if they canceled their contract, we would have to rebuild the business from scratch. The change or cancellation in contract can be caused by a change in management, merger or buyout, which the multi-national companies seem to go through frequently. We prefer to grow organically working with a variety of customers.

"Look in the mirror and you will find out how you see the world"
- A Punjabi Proverb.

Brewing Up A Damn Good Story

> *You can guess a man's intellect by simply saying the word "beer!" and watching his reaction. He is on top of his game if he mumbles some hard to understand words but obviously would love to have a beer. If he has a blank look, make another friend. He is not worth the time.*
>
> *- Manjit Minhas*

Prefer to Work with Family-owned Firms

Perhaps we are biased on this but as a family-owned business, we prefer working with other family-owned companies, wherever possible. The difficulty of working with large companies is that they often have a revolving door of staff and management coming and going. The advantages of working with a family-owned business is that you can always call the owner who is there over the long term and settle any misunderstandings and disputes that may arise. Many times when a new management comes, the first thing they want to do is to put their "stamp" on the business. This often involves discrediting and devaluing whatever was achieved by the previous management. Frequently, large egos, empire building and office politics get in the way of progress. The new management tries to prove itself by throwing the baby out with the bath water.

Stick to What You Know

We are frequently contacted by people who want to make us millions of dollars by opening a restaurant, by starting an airline or by executing a myriad of business ideas. They want us to be their partners - they want us to invest the funds with a promise that they will provide all the "sweat equity". We universally decline the offers because we know nothing about the business they want us to enter. We know the beer and liquor business very well, we own 100% of all our companies and we prefer to stick to what we know. We simply do not have the time or the energy to learn other businesses.

Live Within Your Means

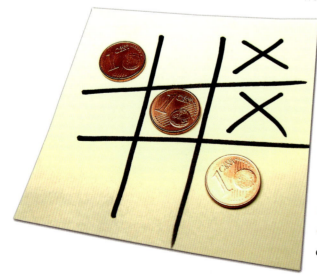

We believe that a business (and a person) should live within their means. Banks will be glad to lend us funds. We have people approaching us on a regular basis to invest in our ventures. We believe that if at all possible, we should own 100% of our businesses and that we should not borrow funds from anybody. We believe in re-investing the profits and playing with our own money. We believe that banks and investors are mainly interested in harvesting the fruits of our labor - without losing their sleep or doing the hard work. Just look at all the high-rise buildings the financial institutions own in every North American city. All of them came from massive profits they made from their customers. We would rather keep all the profits for ourselves. Also, the overhead and time it would take to please the bankers and investors would take us away from paying attention to our core business. We limit our discussion and meetings with our bank managers to paying minimum service fees and earning the highest interest on our money.

Give the Consumers What They Want!

The secret of our business success is the quality of beers we produce. This means we produce beer with taste profiles that match what people want, not what we, our management or even the brewmaster wants. A successful business has to listen to its customers. This applies to all types of industries. There has to be a balance. Providing leadership means having to balance the expertise within the organization to what the customer wants.

Good Guys Do Finish First!

We find it very interesting that the media is always sympathetic to the challenges we face in competing against some of the world's largest companies with billions of dollars at their disposal to stamp us out. They almost always write positive stories about us because we try to be truthful and honest with the media. Usually the public relations department spokespersons of our competitors use double-speak, hide behind the self-serving associations they have created to push their agenda and generally talk like politicians. In contrast, we are the spokespersons for our own company. The media almost always see through our competitors' tactics - they are very intelligent and intuitive about these things. We are our own Public Relations Department, we write our own press releases and we create our own TV commercials. The media sense our honesty and write stories in that spirit.

> *In ancient Babylonia, the father of a bride would supply his new son-in-law with a month's worth of mead, a honey beer. Since they used lunar (moon based) calendar at the time, this month-long beer session came to be known as the "honey month", which changed to "honeymoon" over time.*

- Honeymoon, a popular expression that originated from beer.

Always Have Fun!

We believe that we must constantly create new products and expand to new territories - but perhaps even more importantly, we must have fun along the way. We have found out that without fun, we can not achieve anything. Besides, what other business could be more fun than the beer business?

Taking Care of Mother Earth Is Good Business

We believe that we must take care of the only planet we have. We have found out that taking care of Mother Earth has many benefits - it feels good, it is great for public relations and it is profitable for business.

Let Numbers Do The Talking

Perhaps because of our engineering education, we believe that expressing most things in numbers speaks volumes about their nature and perhaps more importantly, the trend they are going in. As an example, the charts below show production at the Brewery over the years, based on data modeling we have done. This gives us great insight into the successes and failures of the brewery over the years.

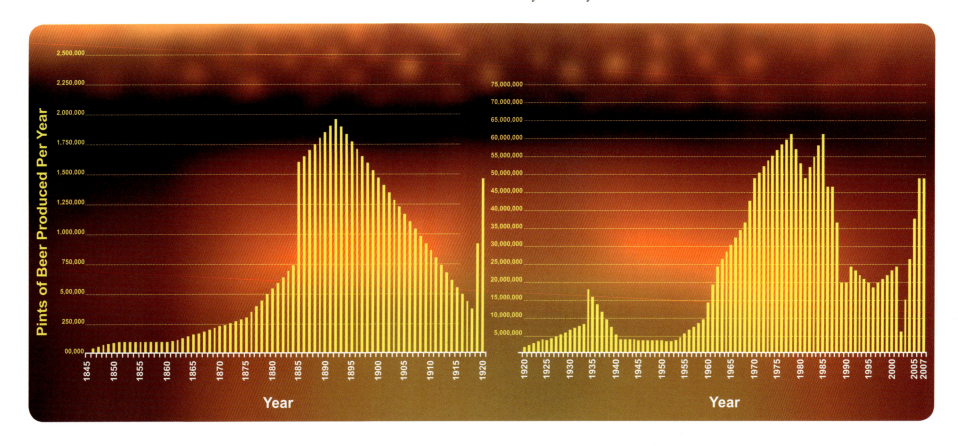

MILESTONES FOR THE MINHAS FAMILY
& ITS BREWING BUSINESS SUCCESS

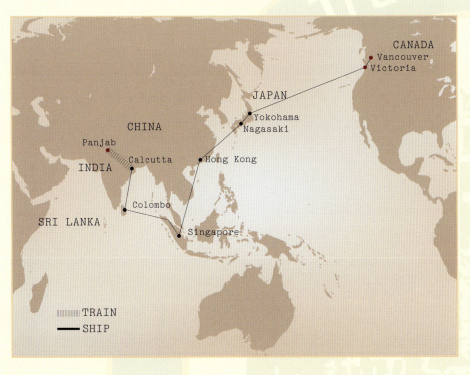

1906

Two brothers of Ravinder and Manjit Minhas' maternal great grandfather migrate from Punjab, India to the Westcoast of Canada. They were one of the very first immigrants from South East Asia to North America. Soon, they are followed by their nephews and nieces – all moving to Vancouver, Vancouver Island and other areas of British Columbia in Canada.

1980

Manjit Minhas is born in Calgary Alberta Canada, being the first born of Moni and Rani Minhas.

1982

Ravinder Minhas is born in Calgary Alberta Canada, being the second and youngest child of Moni and Rani Minhas.

1999

Manjit Minhas introduces the Mountain Crest brands of spirits (Vodka, Canadian Whisky, Rum and Gin) to Alberta, Canada at the age of 19 years The legal drinking age in Alberta is 18 years.

2000

Ravinder Minhas joins his sister Manjit Minhas in the liquor business.

2002, April 13

Manjit and Ravinder Minhas enter the beer business by launching their new brand Mountain Crest Classic Lager that was made at the Minnesota Brewing Company of Minneapolis-St. Paul, Minnesota. This is one of the most successful new brands introduced in Canada in decades. The brand grows at a rapid pace and goes out of stock every summer for the following three years.

2002, June 27

Minnesota Brewery goes bankrupt and is closed. Production is moved to the City Brewery in Lacrosse, Wisconsin.

2003 September

Production of the Mountain Crest Classic Lager and the Classic Pilsner is permanently moved to Joseph Huber Brewery in Monroe. This requires a large capital investment in equipment. Soon, the Brewery's production increases five fold within three years. Many other brands are introduced in Canada, the USA and Japan.

2004

Minhas Creek Classic Lager and other brands are introduced in Manitoba, Canada.

2006, October 3

The brother and sister team of Ravinder (24 years old) and Manjit (26 years old) Minhas purchase the Brewery, thereby becoming the youngest brewery owners in the world. They immediately change the name of the brewery to "Minhas Craft Brewery".

Within the next 1 ½ years, they invest $5 million in capital improvements to the Brewery, including a 50,000 square foot Warehouse and Distribution Center, Clear Malt System, 16 and 24 oz. can lines, new storage, fermentation and ageing tanks, Riverwood Twinstack Can Packaging Machine for making 24 cubes, 30 packs and 36 packs and a new Visitor Center incorporating a Museum, Lazy Mutt Lounge and Gift Center. With the new improvements, the Brewery now has modern and efficient production systems and has doubled its production capability. It is currently equipped to package cans in 12 oz., 16 oz., 24 oz. and 5L; glass in 12 oz., 40 oz. and Sankey Kegs in ½ and ¼ barrels. Minhas Craft Brewery is estimated to have a replacement value of $100 million.

2007 - 2008

New age beverages such as iEnergy, Fermented Malt Beverages and four Craft Beers – Lazy Mutt Farmhouse Ale, 1845 PILS, Swiss Amber Ale and Fighting Billy Bock are launched.

2008

Minhas Creek Classic Lager and other brands are introduced in Saskatchewan, Canada.

Minhas Craft Brewery introduces its brands throughout the Midwest, including Illinois, Ohio, Missouri, Georgia, Wisconsin and Minnesota.

> "You can't grow up in Canada and not love beer and hockey. That is what makes us Canadian."
>
> - Ravinder Minhas

MILESTONES IN THE LIFE OF A BREWERY

1845

The brewery is built on its present site in Monroe by Mr. Bissinger.

The following gives an indication of the time period in which the Brewery was founded:
* James Polk was the 11th President of the US.
* The first US postage stamp was issued.
* The battle of Ferozeshaw in India ended between the British and the Sikhs.

The Brewery in Monroe was started 10 years before the Miller Brewery got its start in Milwaukee Wisconsin, 28 years before the Coors Brewery started in Golden, Colorado and 31 years before the Anheuser-Busch Brewery started in St. Louis, Missouri.

1848-1857

John Knipschildt owns the Brewery.

1848

Wisconsin becomes the 30th state in the US.

1857-1861

George Esser and John Hermann own the Brewery.

1858

The Village of Monroe Wisconsin is incorporated, named after James Monroe, the 5th US President.

1861-1867

John Hermann owns the Brewery.

1867-1868

Captain Edward Ruegger owns the Brewery.

1868-1885

Jacob Hefty owns the Brewery.

1875

Fire burns the city jail adjacent to the brewery; (now a bar called Jailhouse Tap) workers put out the fire by dousing flames with "Green Beer".

1885-1892

Jacob Hefty and Adam Blumer Sr. own the Brewery.

1892-1918

Adam Blumer Sr. owns the Brewery.

1900

Monroe becomes known as the "Swiss Cheese Capital of the World".

1906

The brewery name is changed to the Blumer Brewery.

1918-1938

Fred J. Blumer and his two brothers own the Brewery.

1920

Federal prohibition of alcohol starts throughout the US. In order to survive, the Blumer Brewery changes its name to Blumer Products Corp., and starts producing Golden Glow "near beer", ice cream and soft drinks. Golden Glow becomes very popular and the Brewery prospers, against all odds. Hundreds of other breweries across the USA close down.

1927

Fred J. Blumer and his brothers hire Joseph Huber, a young immigrant from Germany.

1931

Business at the Brewery is very good due to the very popular Blumer's near beer "Golden Glow". As per Prohibition rules, alcohol is required to be boiled off in an equipment called a de-alcoholizer. Alcohol is emptied into Monroe sewers and has to be diluted with 150 gallons of water per minute.

Fred Blumer, the owner of the Brewery, is kidnapped by the mafia and released after a week of captivity. Fred Blumer never talked to anybody about his terrifying experience until a month before his death in 1956.

1933

National prohibition of alcohol is repealed! The Company's name reverts to Blumer Brewing Company. The outlook for the beer industry is very optimistic and the Brewery undergoes major expansion.

1934

A new three floor office building is built on the corner of 14th Avenue and 13th Street in place of the residences of the Hefty and Blumer families.

For the first time in its history, public offering of stock is made consisting of 200,000 shares at $1.20 per share. This news is covered across the country by Associated Press (AP) and the newspapers. Sales in 1933 are $528,234 with a profit of $155,558.

1939

Monroe cheese magnates - Carl O. Marty Jr. and his partners Ralph H. Wenger and Edward Ninneman - purchase the Brewery from the Blumer family.

1941-1947

Carl O. Marty Jr., the local cheese magnate is the sole owner of the Brewery.

1941

The euphoria and optimism that existed in the beer business is waning as small to medium size breweries are struggling to make a profit. Joseph Huber and five other workers agree to operate the Brewery, with Carl O. Marty Jr. providing the funds and leasing the equipment and building.

1941-1957

Carl O. Marty Jr. and his company Monroe Cold Storage convert 35,000 square foot of the Brewery cellar space for cheese storage. Six million pounds of cheese is stored in the second floor and basement of the office building. Producers and dealers of cheese are able to borrow money against the cheese they have stored at the Brewery. In effect, a portion of the Brewery is also operating like a "Cheese Bank".

1947

Joseph Huber acquires the Brewery and the Brewery's name is changed to the Joseph Huber Brewing Company.

Huber brand is introduced, in addition to the Hi Brau and the Golden Glow brands that have been produced for many years.

1953

Fred Huber, Joseph's son, returns home from service in the US Marines and starts working at the brewery helping to boost its sales. Huber beer is introduced in cans.

1957

Joseph Huber announces a $3 per share dividend.

1958

A new 10,000 square foot bottlehouse is built, south of the County Jail. A tunnel is built under the 14th Avenue to bring beer from the Brewhouse across the street underground.

1960

Huber Brewery in Monroe Wisconsin wins the contract to brew Berghoff beer. Herman and Harry Berghoff had started Berghoff Brewery on Grant Avenue in Fort Wayne Indiana back in 1887. They introduced the Berghoff beer to Chicago in 1893; soon after they opened the famous German restaurant "The Berghoff", now the oldest restaurant in Chicago. The Fort Wayne Brewery is sold in 1954 to Falstaff Brewing but the Berghoff family (Herman Jr.) retained the

Berghoff labels and recipes. At the height of its popularity, the Berghoff beer sold over seven million cases per year. The Berghoff recipes and brand were sold to the owners of the Monroe Brewery in 1994. The production of Berghoff beer continues at the Monroe Brewery to this day.

1963

Regal Brau, a German type brew is introduced. It is still being produced.

1967

Rhinelander Brewery was established on 1 Ocala Street, Rhinelander in north Wisconsin in 1852. It closes down in 1967. The Monroe Brewery purchases its flagship brand "Rhinelander" and starts producing it in Monroe Wisconsin. Minhas Craft Brewery is still producing the Rhinelander beer.

TRADITION & HERITAGE THAT CONTINUES...

1969
The Brewery is owned by Joseph Huber, Fred Huber and seven other shareholders.

1972
The Potosi Brewing Company, established in Potosi, Wisconsin in 1852, closes down in 1972. Joseph and Fred Huber and the Brewery in Monroe purchase its recipes and brands - Augsburger, Bohemian Club, Potosi, Van Merritt, Holiday and Alpine, Barrel of Beer and Our Beer brands. They produce and market these brands for many years to come. The Monroe Brewery still makes Potosi beer on occasion for promotional purposes. In 2008, the National Brewery Museum is opened in the previous Potosi Brewery site in Potosi, Wisconsin with much fanfare.

After buying the Augsburger brand, Fred Huber and Hans Kestler change its recipe and introduce it in distinctive green bottles. This was the first super premium craft beer marketed in the US. From 1972 to 1985, it grows steadily selling three million cases annually making it one of the best selling super-premium beers in the Midwest.

1973
The Meister Brau Brewery was established in Chicago in 1891 as the Peter Hand Brewery. It had changed its name to the Meister Brau Brewery in 1967 and invented the light beer. The Meister Brau Light brand and recipe were sold in the late 1960s to the Miller Brewery of Milwaukee. Miller changed the name of the brand to Miller Lite, marketed it heavily, created the Light Beer category and grew it to a major national brand. In 1973, the Meister Brau Brewery of Chicago goes bankrupt. Fred Huber, the owner of the Monroe Brewery and other investors purchase the Meister Brau Brewery and its facilities in Chicago and produce various brands until 1978, at which time they close it down for good. Much of the equipment from this brewery and its brands, such as Old Chicago and Boxer get transferred to the Monroe Brewery.

1975
Braumeister is bought by Huber from G. Heileman Brewing Co. of LaCrosse, Wisconsin. Originally it was a Milwaukee beer.

1977 - 1985
Fred Huber owns the Brewery with various partners. He had acquired majority ownership of brewery upon the death of his father Joseph Huber.

1978
"The Great American Beer Book" published by Caroline House Publishers Inc. of Illinois lists Augsburger as the "best beer brewed in America". Fred Huber is given the ceremonial key by the City of Augsburg, Germany for putting it on the map in the USA. Augsburger Beer is advertised with very popular radio ads starring Hans Kestler, the brewmaster.

1985
Huber Brewery reaches an all time high by producing 250,000 barrels of beer production. The employees at the Brewery work around the clock to keep up with the demand for Augsburger beer, a very popular beer in Chicago and other areas of the Midwest.

To everyone's surprise, Fred Huber sells the Brewery and its brands (including Augsburger, its flagship brand) to MTX Inc., owned by William Smith the former president of Pabst Brewery and R. Craig Werle, also an ex-executive of Pabst for $7.8 Million. Hans Kestler, the brewmaster is let go soon after.

1986
The Brewery makes the country's first Fermented Malt Beverage (FMB) – Savannah Peach and Lemon Coolers.

1988
Another big surprise comes when Smith & Werle sell the Augsburger label to Stroh Brewing, the beer giant from Detroit, Michigan. They plan to close the brewery, unless a suitable buyer is found. They spearhead the Augsburger marketing for Stroh as it is turned into a national brand. With Augsburger now being produced by Stroh in Minneapolis, Minnesota, the production at the Monroe Brewery declines by 60%.

1989
Fred Huber, Hermann Berghoff and a group of investors buy the brewery from MTX Inc for $2.25 million. Berghoff becomes their flagship brand now that Augsburger is gone. Local 744 of the International Brotherhood of Teamsters Union agrees to take a cut in wages and vacations in order to keep the Brewery going.

1991
Media reports claim "Stroh in addition to using barley, hops, yeast and water now use corn and low quality hops". Unconfirmed rumors abound that Stroh never received the correct recipe for Augsburger. Ironically, the Monroe Brewery still has the original Augsburger recipe in its vault. Hans Kestler is re-hired as brewmaster by Fred Huber.

Berghoff beers are sold in 20 states.

1992
A boost in production comes in October 1991 when Huber Brewery starts making beers for the Campagnia Cervecera Victoria Brewery of Nicaragua.

Also, the Brewery starts making Andechs beer, owned by the Benedictine Monks south west of Munich - the first time this beer is produced outside of Germany in its 500 year history.

Huber re-introduces Old Chicago beer in Chicago and exports it to Britain, Paraguay and Argentina.

The Brewery starts making Mystic, juice based non alcoholic beverage for Joseph Victori Wine Company of New York.

1994
The Weinstein-Minkoff family from Madison Wisconsin purchase the Brewery. They invest an additional $1.3 million in capital and introduce new brands.

Berghoff gains regional popularity and both Berghoff Original and Berghoff Dark are named among the Best Beers in the World by *Wine Enthusiast* magazine.

The Berghoff brands are purchased from Herman Berghoff for $ 1.2 million.

1998
Wisconsin Club is introduced. It is exported to Brazil, Panama, England, Russia and France.

2001
The Brewery opens the Founder's Tap Room, a new gift shop and opens for tours after renovations costing $125,000.

2002
The Brewery in Monroe wins seven medals at the World Beer Championships including a Gold for Berghoff Oktoberfest; Silver for Berghoff Original Lager, Berghoff Genuine Dark, Berghoff Famous Bock and Huber Bock and Bronze for Berghoff Classic Pilsner and Huber Premium. Fred Huber dies.

2003
The Brewery stops making Huber returnable bottles. Returnable bottles need to be re-used at least four to five times for it to be economical. Returnable bottles have heavier glass to withstand the high temperature water used for washing and sterilization. The returnable bottles were strong enough to withstand 12 returns but many consumers were not returning them back - they were simply throwing them away and filling landfills and back alleys.

2004
John Kerry, the Presidential candidate for the Democratic party and his election machine rolls into the Brewery. John Kerry enjoys the Berghoff Red Ale while his wife Teresa Heinz Kerry, prefers the Berghoff Solstice Wit.

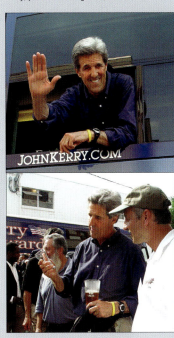

2006, October 3

Ravinder and Manjit Minhas, brother and sister in their 20's purchase the Brewery. They become the youngest brewery owners in the world.

Owners - Present & Past and Their Homegrown Brands

Minhas Craft Brewery

October 3, 2006 to Now - RAVINDER & MANJIT MINHAS

The brother and sister team of Ravinder (24 years old) and Manjit (26 years old) Minhas purchased the Brewery on October 3, 2006.

Ancestors of Ravinder and Manjit Minhas had the distinction of being one of the first people to migrate from India to North America. Traveling by boat, their maternal great-grandfather's two brothers landed in Vancouver, British Columbia on the westcoast of Canada in 1906. Their mother Rani Minhas (nee Parhar) was born in Karnana, Punjab, India and moved to Duncan BC Canada in 1969 when she was a young girl. She finished her education on Vancouver Island. Their father Moni Minhas was born in Daroli Khurd, Punjab, India, (a viillage founded in the early 12TH century) he was raised in New Delhi and completed his engineering degree from Punjab Engineering College in Chandigarh, India. Moni immigrated to the westcoast of Canada in 1976 with only $4 in his pocket, due to the prevailing foreign currency regulations at the time in India. Moni and Rani got married in Paldi on Vancouver Island in BC, Canada in 1976. Soon they moved 1,000 km east to Calgary, Alberta, Canada for Moni to further his engineering education at the University of Calgary. Upon graduation, Moni Minhas worked for 13 years in engineering and administrative positions for an oil company in Calgary. At the same time, Moni and Rani started raising their family and had two children - Manjit, their daughter was born in 1980 and Ravinder, their son, was born in 1982.

Share Certificate (dated 1957) of a Sugar Mill in Punjab, India that represents the first time a Minhas family member had ownership in an incorporated enterprise.

Born and raised in Calgary, Alberta, Manjit and Ravinder went to schools in Calgary and got their introduction to the liquor business around the dinner table as their parents owned and operated the OK Liquor Stores, the largest liquor retailer in Calgary at the time. Ravinder received his Bachelor of Science in Oil and Gas Engineering from the University of Calgary and worked as a Petroleum Engineer for Husky Energy Inc., one of Canada's largest oil exploration companies - working in Unity, Saskatchewan and Calgary, Alberta. Manjit also attended the Universities of Calgary and Regina studying Petroleum Engineering. She also worked for Marathon Oil Company and Devon Energy Corporation for almost a year.

At the age of only 19 years (the legal drinking age in Alberta), Manjit introduced new brands of Vodka, Canadian Whisky, Gin and Rum which were produced and packaged at the Heaven Hill Distillery in Bardstown, Kentucky. This was followed by a successful launch of their Blarney Irish Cream produced in Europe and Alamo tequila, produced in Mexico.

Brewing Up A Damn Good Story

Alamo 100% Blue Agave Reposado Tequila

During the summer of 2002, Manjit and Ravinder entered the beer market in Alberta and gave the big multi-nationals a run for their money with Mountain Crest Classic Lager - brewed and packaged at the Minnesota Brewery located in the Twin Cities. Theirs became the first successful new beer company to enter the Canadian marketplace in decades. After Minnesota Brewery went bankrupt, Ravinder and Manjit moved the production of their brews to the Stephens Point Brewery (Stephens Point, Wisconsin) and the City Brewery (LaCrosse, Wisconsin) for a short time. Then in the summer of 2003, Ravinder started producing his beer at The Joseph Huber Brewery in Monroe, Wisconsin. This required a major upgrade to the facility as several new packaging machines had to be installed. This resulted in the Brewery's production to increase almost five times - going up from 35,000 barrels per year to 200,000 barrels per year within a period of three years.

In late 2004, Manjit founded Minhas Creek Brewing Company in Manitoba and introduced her new flagship brand Minhas Creek Classic Lager. Manjit caused a stir in the Manitoba beer industry by gaining large market share in a very short amount of time with her aggressive marketing and advertising techniques and her pricing strategies. Many beer drinkers welcomed her style of beer as a tasty alternative to the higher priced Canadian beers that dominated the market place.

Ravinder and Manjit Minhas became the first brewers in Canada to voluntarily put a Health Warning on all their beer cans and bottles "MANAGEMENT WARNING: Please do not drink and drive - ever. Expectant mothers should avoid drinking alcoholic products. Enjoy this product responsibly - Respect yourself and others". This resulted in them being given the Alberta Government's Fetal Alcohol Spectrum Disorders (FASD) Recognition Award.

Manjit Minhas has been given several business and industry awards. Some are listed below:

- Top 100 Women Entrepreneurs in Canada

- "Top Growth Entrepreneur" award, *Profit* magazine in Toronto

- Ranked #6 in the "Top 50 Fastest Growing Companies" by *Alberta Venture Magazine*

- Young Achiever Award from the Indo-Canada Chamber of Commerce

- Government of Alberta - Alberta Centennial Medallion Award

- "Up and Coming CEO" from *The National Post*, Canada's National Newspaper

- Canada's Women Executive Network Top 100 Women Entrepreneurs Award

- *Calgary Inc Magazine's* Top 40 Under 40 Award and later a member of its Selection Committee

Ravinder Minhas has received the following business and industry awards :

- Government of Alberta - Alberta Centennial Medallion Award

- FASD (Fetal Alcohol Spectrum Disorders) Recognition Award

- University of Calgary "Graduate of the Last Decade" GOLD Award 2007

- JCI Outstanding Young Calgarian Award

- *Calgary Inc Magazine* and Canada's Top 40 Under 40

- Ernst & Young Entrepreneur of the Year Emerging Entrepreneur Award

- Alberta Chamber of Commerce Marketing Award

Ravinder and Manjit's story has been featured in many publications such as *Macleans Magazine, Canadian Business Magazine, Alberta Venture Magazine, The National Post, The Globe & Mail, The Calgary Herald, The Edmonton Journal, The Toronto Star, The Toronto Sun, The Winnipeg Free Press and the Bar & Beverage Magazine*. Their story of success has also been featured on TV in programs such as the *CBC National, CBC Venture, Careers TV,* and many other news programs in Calgary, Edmonton, Winnipeg and Toronto.

Upon purchasing The Joseph Huber Brewing Co. Inc. on October 3, 2006, Ravinder and Manjit Minhas changed its name to Minhas Craft Brewery. This was followed with a capital investment of $5 million - by far the biggest capital investment plan in the long history of the Brewery. This included adding a 50,000 square foot Warehouse & Distribution Center, 24 oz. (710 mL) can filler line, Riverwood Twinstack Can Packaging Machine to make 12 pack fridge pack, 24 pack cube, 30 pack and 36 packs, new visitor center with a museum, gift store and the Lazy Mutt Lounge, Clear Malt System, new storage and fermentation tanks, Minhas Craft Brewery Guest House and new malt silos. More than 20 new products were introduced in new territories including Japan, the Midwest in the USA and in various parts of Canada.

Owners before October 2006

The Brewery in Monroe has been owned over the last 163 years by some of the most prominent citizens of the area. They were 1st or 2nd generation immigrants, tracing their origins from Switzerland, France, Britain, Germany and Denmark.

Monroe Brewing Company (1845-1906)

1845- 1848 Mr. Bissinger

He founded the Brewery at its present site. At the time, it was a winter operation consisting of a Brew Kettle and could only make a few hundred barrels per year.

1848- 1857 John M. Knipschildt (born 1805)

On October 30, 1841, John M. Knipschildt was living in the Lee County in North Central Illinois when he made his declaration to become a citizen of the USA and broke his alliance with "Frederick William the Fourth, King of Prussia". Shortly after Wisconsin became the 30th state in the United States, Mr. Knipschildt purchased the Brewery in 1848. Within two years, he had invested $1,000 in the Brewery and produced 366 barrels per year. The Brewery was hand powered and employed two people who were paid $50 per year. Wood and coal were used for fuel. Mr. Knipschildt was also a Treasurer and a Trustee of the Green County.

Berwery in the late 1800's

1857 - 1861 George Esser and John Hermann

The malting of barley was also done right at the Brewery. In 1858, Mr. Esser and Mr. Hermann built the underground beer storage cellars as there were no ice or mechanically controlled cellars at that time. Also, lager beer was produced for the first time during their ownership - prior to this only ales were brewed. Winter was still the only time brewing took place. By 1860, the Brewery's production had increased many fold and the Brewery had nearly a 100% marketshare in the Green County and within a 25 mile radius area. Interestingly, John Hermann was actually living right at the Brewery.

> *I love the beer business. Where else could you package loads of happiness in millions of bottles?*
>
> - Ravinder Minhas

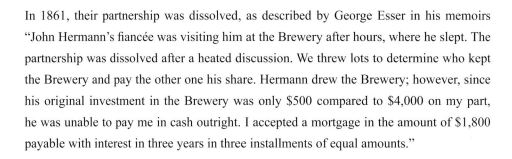

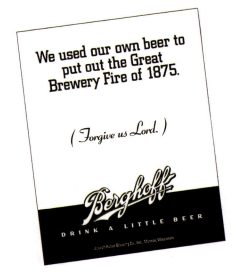
Jacob Hefty

In 1861, their partnership was dissolved, as described by George Esser in his memoirs "John Hermann's fiancée was visiting him at the Brewery after hours, where he slept. The partnership was dissolved after a heated discussion. We threw lots to determine who kept the Brewery and pay the other one his share. Hermann drew the Brewery; however, since his original investment in the Brewery was only $500 compared to $4,000 on my part, he was unable to pay me in cash outright. I accepted a mortgage in the amount of $1,800 payable with interest in three years in three installments of equal amounts."

1861 - 1867 John Hermann

There were still only two people employed earning $65 per month. But now, a horse was used to power the brewery and 400 barrels were produced per year. John Hermann married his Swiss fiancée on August 16, 1861 in Monroe.

1867 - 1868 Captain Edward Ruegger (born October 18, 1836, died in early 1900s)

Captain Ruegger migrated in 1854 from La Havre, in northwest France accompanied by his parents. A Swiss by origin, he became a prominent citizen of Monroe and had various business interests including a wagon building and a fire and life insurance company. He owned the brewery for two years. His public service included serving as fire chief and sheriff for the city of Monroe as well as the president of the Monroe Rifle Club. He and his wife Sophia (nee Shober) had nine children - all born in Monroe.

1868 - 1885 Jacob Hefty (born April 15,1835, died 1892)

Jacob Hefty was born in Canton Glarus, Switzerland, and came to Green County in 1847. He was the first person of his nationality to learn the English language in the town of New Glarus. He married Catherine Blumer in 1857 and had six children. He distributed beer under the "Monroe" label. The Brewery produced 1,200 barrels annually and employed four males, with an annual payroll of $3,000 per year. One horse still powered the Brewery. On a very cold night on December 27, 1875, there was a terrible fire that destroyed the Brewery. The fire was put out using "green beer". The loss was $12,000 and the Brewery was only insured for $5,000.

In 1884, the Brewery was producing 3,000 barrels and had revenue of $12,000.

1885 -1892 Jacob Hefty and Adam Blumer Sr. (born April 1, 1844, died 1918)

Jacob Hefty was joined by his brother-in-law Adam Blumer Sr. as a 50% owner in 1885. Adam Blumer Sr. and his family would remain part of the Brewery for the next 62 years.

1892 - 1906 Adam Blumer Sr.

In 1892, Adam Blumer Sr. became the sole owner of the Brewery. He was a native of Switzerland and was the youngest of 16 children. His parents were pioneer settlers in Washington township, just outside of Monroe, Wisconsin when they started farming upon their arrival from Switzerland on April 3, 1849 at the Port of New York. Their tract consisted of 240 acres. They lived in a log house and had to contend with all the hardships encountered in pioneer farming. The young man attended the district school; however, with the death of his father in 1855, he was obliged to assume his share of the responsibilities in the running of the family farm.

Later the entire management of the old homestead fell into his hands. He applied himself with energy and ambition. His firm was soon known as one of the most successful farms of the time in the county, extending to 476 acres. He started a cheese manufacturing enterprise in 1862, which he continued for the next 30 years. He began dairying and cheese making with a herd of 25 cows. In a few years he enlarged the herd to almost a hundred. Adam Blumer was one of the first in the area to succeed in large scale dairy farming in Green County.

Adam Blumer Sr. was married on March 23, 1865 to Miss Margaret Hefty and had seven children. He retired from farming and moved to Monroe in 1891, later becoming an Alderman.

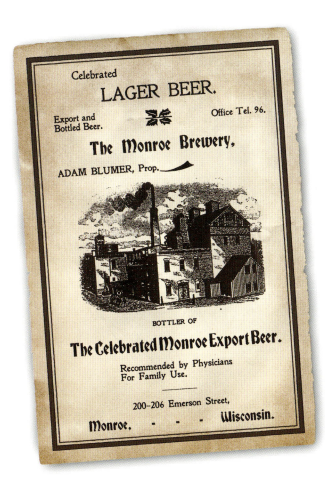

Adam Blumer Sr.

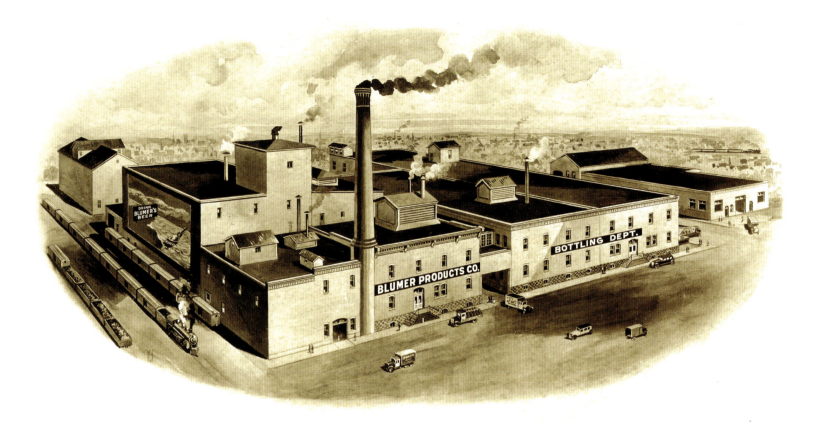

Blumer Brewing Company (1906 - 1947)

1906- 1918 Adam Blumer Sr.

In 1906, the name of the Brewery was changed to Blumer Brewing Company. When Adam Blumer, Sr. took over the brewery in 1892, it was a "one-horse" operation but during his years of ownership, the plant was rebuilt and equipped throughout with modern machinery. When he was done, it was a modern brewery in every respect and it became a major regional brewery - a distinction it retains to this day. He was so popular that when he was dying, his name was placed on the ballot without opposition. He was also a long time member of the County Board of Supervisors.

1918 - 1938 Fred J. Blumer (born 1880, died 1956)

Fred J. Blumer took over the ownership of the Brewery upon the death of his father Adam Blumer Sr. Under the management of Fred J. Blumer and his brothers Jacob C. and Adam Jr. Blumer, the Brewery expanded and proved to be one of the most up-to-date breweries in Wisconsin. At this time the Blumer Brewing Company had a yearly output of 12,000 barrels. When Fred and his brother took over the brewery, it only produced around 1,500 barrels a year. The brothers brought in electric equipment and practically rebuilt the brewery.

Fred J. Blumer

Fred J. Blumer was active in the development of Monroe and the surrounding area. He married Bessie Dean, of Milwaukee, Wisconsin, a daughter of James and Eva Dean, on June 24, 1898. They had one daughter Marion Blumer. He was also Vice President of the First National Bank of Monroe for many years. Despite all the improvements Fred Blumer made at the Brewery, he took over the Brewery at the worst time in the brewing history of the USA. A year after taking over the business to which he had dedicated his life, the brewery business became illegal with the onset of Prohibition of Alcohol throughout the US.

Blumer Brewing Company changed its name to Blumer Products Company in 1920. In order to survive, it started making ice cream, non alcoholic beer and started distributing Case tractors, separators, silo fillers, and road machinery. At the Blumer Products Company, they came up with the Blumer's Golden Glow Near Beer, which became extremely popular. Also, before the 1920s, there was no concept of the branding of beers. Fred Blumer and his team introduced modern advertising and marketing techniques for the first time.

The "Noble Experiment" as the National Prohibition of alcohol was called, failed miserably. On April 7, 1933, the Prohibition law was repealed and the Blumer's Golden Glow "Real Beer" was re-introduced. The brewing industry was optimistic of a great future. Fred J. Blumer invested a lot of capital to expand the capacity of the brewery. However, the next five years proved to be difficult years to make a profit. On January 24, 1938, Fred J. Blumer resigned and announced a new Board of Directors led by Carl O. Marty, his brother Robert F. Marty and other cheese magnates from Monroe and Milwaukee.

1938 - 1947 Carl O. Marty Jr. (born 1899, died 1979)

In 1938, Carl O. Marty, the big cheese magnate of Monroe, bought the majority ownership in Blumer Brewery partly for its large cold storage space for cheese. Carl O. Marty and his brother Robert F. were visionaries and naturalists. They created the "Waldorf of the Wilderness", the Northern Aire Hotel and Spa in the Three Lakes area of northern Wisconsin, fronting the Big Stone and Deer Lake. They have been credited with ushering in the "Golden Era" of the Northwoods Resort industry.

First National Bank - Augsburger bottle. Amcore Bank, the current banker of the Minhas Craft Brewery bought the First National Bank of Monroe in 1977.

Carl O. Marty

Carl O. Marty Cheese Factory.

On March 30, 1944, Carl O. Marty sold part of his interest in the beer operation to a group of stock holders. He named Joseph Huber as the president and manager of the brewery while Carl O. Marty remained the president of the Monroe Cold Storage, Inc. It was estimated that the cheese curing and storage of the cold storage part of the plant was at six million pounds of cheese.

Marty organized the Swiss Cheese Corporation of America and the Capital Cheese Company. His offices and storage facilities occupied the main brewery building for the next three decades, until the death of Carl O. Marty in 1969 and his brother Robert F. Marty in 1970. The Green County Cheese Factory was also located adjacent to the Brewery property. The Cheese Factory was shut down in the 1980s; however, its three story building remained part of the Brewery property. The building was finally torn down in 2007 to make room for the 50,000 square foot Minhas Craft Brewery's Warehouse & Distribution Center.

Joseph Huber Brewing Company (1947 - 2006)

Joseph Huber (born November 8, 1893, died February 8, 1977)

In 1947, when Carl O. Marty sold his brewery business interest to Joseph Huber, he changed the name to The Joseph Huber Brewing Company. He would lease the property and buildings from Carl O. Marty and the Swiss Cheese Corp. for the next 20 years, when he finally purchased the real estate in 1967. Carl O. Marty continued to operate the Swiss Cheese Corp. from the adjacent property.

Born in Pirking, Germany, Joseph Huber was the son of Michael and Katherine G. Huber. He was a decorated soldier for the German Army, having served in the World War I. He came to the US in 1923 and settled in Yankton, South Dakota. He lived there for a year, then he worked for the Blatz Brewing Company in Milwaukee before coming to Monroe in 1927.

In Monroe, he was employed by the Blumer Brewing Company. Joseph Huber saw the brewery grow as he advanced from a brewery worker for the Blumer Brewing Company to the president of his own company.

Joseph Huber's wife, the former Rose Braml, was also a native of Germany coming to America in 1923. They were married in Monroe on April 11, 1931, in St. Victor's Catholic Church. Both Joseph and Rose had attended the same school in Weiding, Bavaria.

Joseph Huber is still remembered fondly by the residents of Monroe as somebody who was an active member of the community. He was known also for having a very friendly demeanor and being a hard working entrepreneur.

When Joseph Huber died in 1977, he was survived by his wife, Rose; a son, Fred, a daughter Mary Ann Cummins of Santa Monica, California; 11 grand children; and two great-great grandchildren. Joseph Huber is buried in Monroe at the Calvary Cemetery.

Huber Regular and Huber Bock were introduced in 1947 by Joseph Huber. After more than 60 years, they are still going strong - this is despite the fact that they were sold in "returnable" bottles for a very long time which have since been discontinued in the interest of preserving the environment. He also introduced Regal Brau, a German style beer in 1963 and Wisconsin Club a few years later. These brands continue to sell after 45 years.

Joseph Huber

1977 - 1985 Fred Huber (born December 22, 1931, died January 7, 2002)

Fred Huber was born in Monroe, Wisconsin to Joseph and Rose Huber. He graduated from the Monroe High School and the Loras College in Dubuque, Iowa where he was known on the football field as the "Golden Toe from Monroe". He was raised around the Monroe Brewery, so it was natural for him to start working full time for his father Joseph Huber in 1953. After working at the Monroe Brewery for several decades Fred moved to Chicago and resurrected the Peter Hand Brewery in 1973. He remained the vice president of the Brewery in Monroe. He became president of the Joseph Huber Brewery in Monroe in 1977 upon the death of his father Joseph Huber. With the exception of four years from 1985-89, he continued running the Brewery until 1994 when he sold it to the Weinstein-Minkoff family of Madison, Wisconsin.

Fred Huber was married to Joan and had seven children. He later divorced, re-married and lived out his last years in Lake View, Illinois, on the Lake Michigan near Chicago.

It is fair to say that Fred Huber is one of the main reasons that there is still a Brewery in Monroe and that it did not shut down like the hundreds of breweries that closed down in the 1970s and 80s across America. Fred Huber was a promoter, a visionary, a maverick entrepreneur and a rescuer of several now defunct breweries and beer brands. He was a great story teller and a likeable man. He liked living "large" and loved to socialize with the rich and the famous, including the legendary coach Mike Ditka of the NFL's Chicago Bears. He also had a knack of bringing in a variety of investors, partners and financial backers for the Brewery over the decades.

Fred Huber

Here is a partial list of Fred Huber's accomplishments, proving that he was decades ahead of his time:

- He helped create the Augsburger brand and its recipe, the first craft super premium beer in the US. During his ownership, the Brewery reached its maximum throughput of 250,000 barrels in the 1980s in its entire history.

- He aggressively marketed the Augsburger brand, with the radio ads featuring the legendary brewmaster Hans Kestler and the now famous line "Drink a Little Beer".

- He resurrected and introduced Berghoff Beer in bottles and sold it in 20 states.

- He rescued beer brands from various now defunct breweries such as the Potosi Brewery of Potosi, Wisconsin, Peter Hand Brewery of Chicago, Illinois and the Rhinelander Brewery of Rhinelander, Wisconsin.

- He was the first to export beer from the Brewery to Brazil, France, Russia, Nicaragua, Panama, Japan, China, the UK and many other countries.

In 1985. Fred Huber stunned everybody in the community and the industry when he sold the Brewery to Bill Smith, the former president of Pabst Brewery and Craig Werle, another senior Pabst executive. However, this would not end his involvement with the Brewery. He would purchase the Brewery back in 1989 and run it for another five years till 1994.

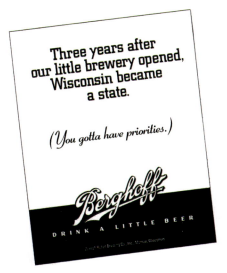

> *Everybody believes in something.*
> *I believe I should have another beer.*
>
> *- Sign posted in the*
> *Visitor Center of the Minhas Craft Brewery*

Brewing Up A Damn Good Story

Michael Jackson

Here is a tribute to Fred Huber written by Michael Jackson, the legendary craft beer expert, and host of the popular TV documentary "The Beer Hunter" that aired in 15 countries:

Tribute to Fred Huber upon his death by Michael Jackson

Even today, many Americans believe that Wisconsin is the beer state. One of the last independent family brewers in Wisconsin was Fred Huber. He was also one of the first brewers to welcome -- and assist -- my pioneering efforts to write informed books on beer for the consumer.

Despite his manifestly good intentions, he nearly brought my career to a premature end. In about 1980, driving me to his brewery, he was enthusing about a new beer, and was momentarily distracted from the road. He turned into a freeway when an oncoming car, being driven fast, was very close. Had the driver of the other car not been alert, it would have slammed into the front passenger side of ours. "I can see the headlines now," observed a chastened Fred: "'Brewer kills world's leading beer writer.'" Having survived, I was grateful for the sobriquet.

This near-miss did not dim his enthusiasm for driving me. After dinner at a Chicago tavern called the Golden Ox, he somehow persuaded all the staff physically to deny me access to a phone. I wanted to call a cab, but he was determined to chauffeur me home. First, though, he had to finish a card game of interminable complexity. Every time I mentioned that I had an early flight the next day, he sent over another glass of beer. On that occasion, he was ordering an imported German Weissbier. Fred had visions of being the first brewer in the US to revive wheat beers, but he never quite managed it.

Fred also had visions of achieving a substantial presence in the Chicago market. He collaborated with the famous Berghoff restaurant for a time, but the resultant beers were a hard sell in the on-premise market. "Why should I stock a beer that advertises another restaurant?" was a typical response. It might work in a smaller, cozier, city, but Chicagoland is a robustly competitive place.

He tried to rescue the city's Peter Hand Brewery, with a crisply hoppy beer called Van Merritt. The Windy City remained stubbornly loyal to Heileman's Old Style, from LaCrosse, Wisconsin. It took even Budweiser decades to shift that obstacle.

For some years, Fred retained the ambition of launching a hoppier Van Merritt at his family brewery in Monroe, Wisconsin. Another Chicago brand, Augsburger, had found its way (via Potosi, Wisconsin) to Monroe. Inspired by an encounter with a German brewer, Fred Huber turned Augsburger into the hoppiest US lager of its time. "Augsburger embraces the brooding bitterness of Spalt with the spicy finish of Hallertau," commented my 1982 "Pocket Guide to Beer." As a "domestic super-premium," Augsburger won a reputation not only in Chicago, but nationally. It was his greatest success.

I never quite stopped expecting new beers from Fred Huber. Then, few days ago, he died. At the memorial service, his son John began with a litany of brands that had at one time or another been Huber's:

Alps, Andechs, Augsburger, Bavarian Club, Bohemian Club, Braumeister, Dempsey's, Golden Glow, Old Chicago, Old Crown, Old German, Peter Hand, Regal Brau, Rhinelander, Van Merritt, Wisconsin Club, Wisconsin Gold Label, Zodiac.

Fred was entrepreneurial, charming, cosmopolitan and urbane but his family connections in Germany stood him in good stead in rural Bavaria. It was an extraordinary coup to obtain a license to brew the beers of the Benedictine Monastery of Andechs.

Fred at one stage sold the brewery, then bought it back. He always had a new idea, some fresh dream to discuss. His profligacy with ideas reflected his generosity. When he was not sending me beers, he was loading me with the other products of America's Dairyland. How many wheels of Wisconsin Jack could one man eat, let alone roll through O'Hare and Heathrow?

> "When I wake up in our Brewery's Guest House, I love the smell of malt and hops. It is a tell-tale sign of victory – victory of good beer against average beer."
>
> - Ravinder Minhas

Brewing Up A Damn Good Story

1985 - 1989 Bill Smith and Craig Werle (MTX Inc.)

When Smith and Werle (through their company MTX Inc. of Milwaukee, Wisconsin), took over the Brewery, it was producing at its peak capacity, and Augsburger was a very popular craft brew in the Midwest. They introduced Savannah FMBs (Flavored Malt Beverages), the first ones to introduce beverage of this type in North America. Mike's Hard Lemonade, Smirnoff Ice and many other FMBs that are popular today, were to come a couple of decades later. They also changed the corporate culture at the Brewery. This included the departure of the legendary brewmaster Hans Kestler.

In 1988, Smith and Werle stunned the community and the industry by selling the Augsburger brand to Stroh Brewing Company, then one of the five largest brewing companies in the USA. With the sale of Augsburger, the Brewery lost 60% of its volume. Smith and Werle announced their intention to close the Brewery. Interestingly, Stroh merged with Pabst in a few years and to this day, the Augsburger brand is owned by Pabst Brewing Company.

1989 - 1994 Fred Huber

Fred Huber with his partners purchased the Brewery in 1989 for a reported $2.3 million. Fred would later disclose that the reason he sold the Brewery in 1985 was that he was burnt out. With Herman Berghoff, owner of the famous Chicago restaurant, as one of his partners, he introduced the Berghoff brand of craft beers and the Mystic line of juice based beverages. He also brought back the famous brewmaster Hans Kestler, who had moved to work at a Hawaii based Brewery. However, the Huber Brewery had large debt and continued to generate losses. In 1994, Fred Huber and his partners sold the Brewery to the Weinstein-Minkoff family of Madison.

Steve Preston

1994 - 2006 Weinstein-Minkoff Family

The Weinstein-Minkoff family based in Madison had a long association with the Monroe Brewery. For many decades, their company General Beer distributed the Brewery's products throughout Wisconsin. They were also investors in the Brewery over the years. The family purchased the Brewery in Monroe in 1994 and injected sizeable capital to upgrade it. Over the next 12 months, they modernized the Brewery, and increased its capacity. Dan Weinstein, Steve Preston, Bob Royko and the senior staff provided the much needed stability at the Brewery after the turbulent 80s and early 90s when the future of the brewery was anything but certain. During this time, various new lines and flavors of beers and sodas were introduced. The Berghoff Family of beers was also expanded.

In 2003, the Brewery started to make beers for Ravinder Minhas for export to Alberta, Canada on a contract basis. Ravinder Minhas also invested in additional can packaging equipment to expand the Mountain Crest line and other brands. This new arrangement increased the production of the Brewery by five times.

By 2005, the beer exported to Alberta made up 85% of the Brewery's total production. The Minhas Family purchased 100% interest in the Brewery on October 3, 2006 and changed the name of the Brewery to Minhas Craft Brewery.

Perhaps the biggest contribution Weinstein-Minkoff family made to the future of the Brewery was that they brought in senior management staff who are the best in the beer business. They continue to provide leadership at the Brewery to this day. The team is led by Gary Olson, the President. Gary Olson had worked in senior management positions at Pepsi and the Minnesota Brewery before coming to the Monroe Brewery. He has implemented many operational improvements at the Brewery. He also has deftly managed the massive capital investment that the new ownership has injected into the Brewery.

" When I land in a new city, I first taste their local beer. From that I can tell a lot who I am going to be dealing with and what kind of trip it is going to be. "

- Ravinder Minhas

Office and management staff at the Minhas Craft Brewery.

Brewing Up A Damn Good Story

Damn Good Beer "DGB" Vehicle, a customized hybrid of Hummer, Cadillac Escalade and Lambo doors that is extensively used for marketing of the Mountain Crest Classic Lager brand.

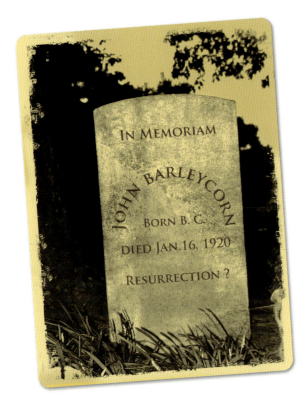

Miserable Failure of a "Noble Experiment"

Prohibition - 13 Years Of Legislated Hell

The 18th Amendment to the US Constitution, brought in 1920, banned the manufacture, sale, and transportation of all types of alcohol, including beer. The "Volstead Act" passed at the same time named after Rep. Andrew J. Volstead of Minnesota, further defined alcohol as all beverages that had more than 0.5% alcohol. Brought in after years of lobbying by religious and political groups (including the Temperance Movement, the "Dries" and the Anti Saloon League) and helped by the post-World War I bias of the general public against the German-Americans who owned most of the breweries - all breweries across America had to stop selling or brewing beer after midnight January 16, 1920. The National Prohibition of alcohol also called "The Noble Experiment" was undertaken to reduce crime and corruption, solve social problems, reduce the tax burden created by prisons, and improve health and hygiene in America. In 1920, all the 1,400 breweries across America were put out of business.

The so called "Noble Experiment" was a miserable failure on all counts: innocent people suffered; organized crime grew their empires; the police, courts, and politicians became increasingly corrupt; disrespect for the law grew; and the per capita consumption of alcohol increased dramatically. Mafia gangs controlled the alcohol business throughout the country. The "Company" led by Al Capone, his enemy Bugs Moran and many others raked in hundreds of millions of dollars and controlled tens of thousands of "speakeasies". Al Capone controlled not only all illicit commerce in Illinois - from alcohol to gambling to prostitution - but also the majority of the politicians, including most police commissioners. By the end of the decade, organized crime was so "organized" they held a national convention in Atlantic City. Even when the chairman of the board, Mr. Capone, took an enforced vacation in 1931 (jailed for income tax evasion and not for illegal liquor trade), his associates continued with the "Company's Business" and managed the "Protection Racket".

When Prohibition started in 1920, the Blumer Brewery Company responded, like many other breweries by introducing "near beer". It was made by first making "real beer" and then boiling off the alcohol using a "distillation" like equipment. The boiled alcohol was then discarded into the sewage system, under supervision of the federal alcohol agents. The City of Monroe had to dilute the alcohol with a lot of water so it did not damage the sewage system.

> *Prohibition makes you want to cry into your beer, and denies you the beer to cry into.*
>
> Source: Don Marquis, 1878-1937,
> American journalist

Anheuser-Busch came up with a near beer called "Bevo", Pabst came up with "Pablo", Miller brewed "Vivo", and Schlitz brewed "Famo"; however, a more appropriate name for all these beers could have been "Crappo". These "near beers" did not taste all that good as the de-alcoholizing process destroyed the taste of the beer. Faced with the horrible tasting "near beer", Americans turned to homebrewing in a big way. By some estimates, over 20 million barrels of beer were homebrewed per year - almost the same amount of legal beer made before prohibition. In some cities, so much homebrew was being made that sewer systems were choked beyond function by the onslaught of spent hops.

A poet painted the following picture of the Prohibition era:

Mother's in the kitchen, washing out the jugs;

Sister's in the pantry, bottling the suds;

Father's in the cellar, mixing up the hops;

Johnny's on the porch, watching for the cops

Old Case Tractor in Monroe area, probably sold by the Blumer Products Company.

This homebrewing revolution was sustained with the eager assistance of merchants who sold malt extracts for "baking." Businesses thrived by selling equipment and other supplies to make liquor. Advertising and selling malt syrups without running afoul of the law posed an interesting challenge. The Malt Syrup packages frequently included instructions "How not to turn the malt syrup into beer as it is against the law". Of course, that was exactly what the homebrewers were doing with the Malt Syrup. And with Malts made for baking like "Nitecap" and "Pilzenbaur", everybody knew what it was meant for.

The homemade beer and liquor also caused poisoning. According to the US Public Health Service, 11,700 people died from imbibing poisonous liquors in 1927. Embalming fluid, antifreeze, and rubbing alcohol were also used to make homemade liquors.

Blumer Brewery survived prohibition by selling "near bear" and ice cream.

It is believed that like most breweries across the country, the Monroe Brewery also made spiked beer during Prohibition. Although by no means prevalent due to strict fines and fear of censure of the "near beer" license, not all the alcohol recovered from de-alcoholizing the beer was drained away. The "near beer" got bottled and the alcohol went to Chicago with the beer where it was re-mixed in the "speakeasies". It is reported that a lookout tower in the Monroe Courthouse was used from where a worker gave the truck loaded with "near beer" and the illegal alcohol a clear signal to depart for Chicago by shining a light if he could not see a federal inspector approaching the Brewery.

> *Near beer is sold here,
> but no beer is sold near here.*

- A popular prohibition period phrase

It was common for bartenders at the "speakeasies" to toss a shot of alcohol into "near beer", just to give it some extra zing. As someone pointed out at that time "This is a crime against both beer and humanity". A speakeasy was an establishment that surreptitiously sold alcoholic beverages during the Prohibition years. The term came from a patron's manner of ordering alcohol without raising suspicion - a bartender would tell a patron to be quiet and "speak easy".

In the words of one beer lover who suffered through the times of "near beer", "A person who called it near beer was a pretty poor judge of distance." On April 7, 1933, after 13 years and a few months, prohibition ended nationwide with the amendment to the Volstead Act defining alcohol as a beverage that contained more than 3.2% alcohol by weight, instead of the previous 0.5% alcohol limit. This was passed under the then President of the USA Franklin D. Roosevelt, who commented after signing the Amendment "I believe that this would be a good time for a beer!". This made beer legal across US as long as it contained a maximum of 3.2% alcohol by weight (4% alcohol by volume). It is interesting to note that to this day "light beers" contain around 3.2% alcohol by weight. "Regular" beer, wine or spirits would not be legal for another 6 months when finally the 18th Amendment to the US constitution that brought in the prohibition of alcohol in the first place was repealed with the passing of the 21st Amendment. In the 220 years history of the US Constitution, the 18th Amendment remains the only one to have been repealed.

President of the USA Franklin D. Roosevelt (1933)

FOR YOUR HEALTH ——— DRINK
GOLDEN GLOW A SPECIAL BREW.
BLUMER PRODUCTS CO.   PHONE 96

Late March and early April of 1933 was an exciting time in the brewing industry as making 'real beer" was now legal. Blumer Brewing Company was no exception. Newspaper articles from the Monroe Evening Times are given below to give the reader a flavor of the times:

> *How important is beer to the happiness of people?*
> *Have you ever gone to a party where there is no alcohol?*
> *Nothing to oil the conversation with and downright boring!*
> *Even the hors d'oeuvres do not taste good.*
>
> - Ravinder Minhas

THE MONROE TIMES

Monroe Evening Times March 23, 1933

BUSY "OPENING NIGHT" PLANNED FOR BREWERY LICENSE HERE, READY TO SHIP 11 P.M., APRIL 6

The hour of 11 o'clock Thursday night, April 6, loom as a busy one at the plant of the Blumer Products Company, Monroe.

A federal license to produce and to bottle "real" beer has been received at the office of the local concern, Fred J. Blumer, President of the company, announced today, and it is his understanding that the first release of 3.2 per cent beer, permitted under federal law effective yesterday, may be made from breweries in the central time zone at 11:00 on the night of April 6.

For some weeks, officers of the Blumer Company have anticipated the legalization of beer in April and have planned their manufacture in such a way that they will be ready to meet all demands at the "zero hour".

Carloads Orders Received

Carload lot orders for Blumer beer are already on file and feverish activity is expected the night of April 6 as trucks are loaded and preparations made to ship immediately by rail.

Local "taverns" licensed by that time are expected to be set for retail dispensing as soon as a truck can make a trip from the brewery to the "tavern" and a period of nocturnal celebration of the end of the dry era is expected.

Mr. Blumer anticipates strict enforcement of the rule that no beer leave breweries before the "zero hour" in order to prevent "gun jumping" on retail sales. A federal inspector is expected at the brewery within the near future to gauge and make measurements as bottling of "real beer" is started.

Brewing Up A Damn Good Story

THE MONROE TIMES

Monroe Evening Times April 7, 1933

CROWD WATCHES AS TRUCKS ROLL FROM BREWERY AT 12:01

Cheers and a roar of big truck, spectators swinging out of the Blumer Brewery property welcomed New Beer' Day in Monroe at 12:01 this morning. The cheers were from part of the throng of curious townspeople who milled about the brewery block for more than an hour before and after the "zero hour" for release of newly legalized 3.2 per cent beer. Yesterday afternoon, trucks from far and near began to take up all available parking spaces near the brewery. The more fortunate ones were permitted to occupy driveways on the brewery property, where they were filled and poised ready to speed away as the hour of 12:01 arrived.

A Lot Of Beer!

Early this afternoon Fred J. Blumer, president of the Blumer Products Company, estimated that 350,000 bottles and 6,500 gallons of beer in kegs had left the company's brewery since 12:01 this morning. About 70 trucks have been loaded. The number of bottles is equal to about 14,582 cases!

Plenty Of Police

Police Chief Jerome H. Schwaiger and Motorcycle Officer Emil Boesch kept traffic moving in the brewery vicinity and at "zero hour" time Assistant Chief A. E. Mitchell joined the detail to help block off regular travel in the vicinity so trucks could make fast getaways without accident. Inside and around the plant were Sheriff Fred W. Faeser and Deputies Myron West and Bismurk Slcklnger on duty to guard against possible holdup or moves by hijackers. Brewery officials stated today that everything moved smoothly and that no reports had come of any trucks being hijacked. Eagerness to taste the new brew was amusingly revealed by some buyers of cases who grabbed, opened and sampled bottles before the cases had been safely stowed in autos. After a few convincing swigs the buyers hurriedly drove away for more leisurely consumption.

THE MONROE TIMES

Monroe Evening Times April 7, 1933

Memorable Night

To the spectators of the unusual brewery drama the night will long live in memory. Whereas in the old days beer was a common beverage and its manufacture and shipment raised no special curiosity, the official drought of 13 years lent rare color to the whole beer business and its official resumption whetted public interest in it as it may never again be whetted.

As midnight neared, truck motors began to hum and at 12:01 the gates were flung open and, to the accompaniment of cheers, and the sounding of auto horns, the trucks moved out. The first went to the Eisenhower agency in Freeport. A laugh came from the crowd as the familiar Eisenhower Austin car bounced out of the gate behind trucks that towered high above it.

Some Back For Refills

As soon as the driveways were cleared of the filled trucks, empty ones moved in for filling. And some of the trucks that left at 12:01 were back shortly after daylight for refills. The grind of big trucks was heard on highways leading to the outskirts of the city all through the night. The clutter of cases being filled rang out through the dark hours at both the brewery and at the Einbeck distributing plant, where Monroe consumers lined up for cases. Through the windows of the shipping rooms at the brewery, cases could be seen piled nearly ceiling high. Bottling activities have been under way for a week in anticipation of the big first day rush.

Loading of freight cars began on the company's siding early today and this afternoon the first rail shipments pulled out. The range of travel by the trucks carrying Blumer's beer was wide. One shipment went to Minneapolis, another as far south as Champaign and Urbana in Illinois. Others to Chicago, Milwaukee and farther North.

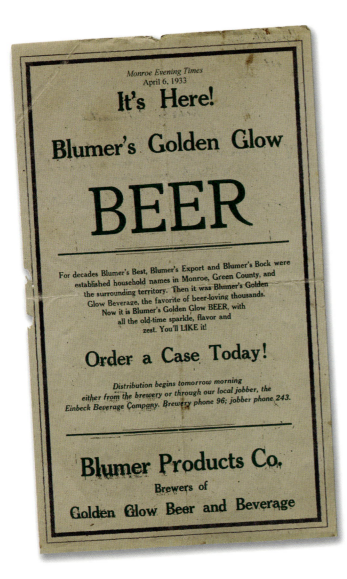

The State of Wisconsin allowed beer to be sold starting April 7, 1933 just after midnight. Here is our Brewery's ad in the local newspaper Monroe Evening Times.

Lasting effects of Prohibition

Prohibition changed the beer industry forever in many respects.

- The 1933 ratification of the Twenty-first Amendment gave the states the right to restrict or ban the purchase or sale of alcohol. This led to a patchwork of laws, in which alcohol may be legally sold in some but not all towns or counties within a particular state. After the repeal of the national constitutional amendment, some states continued to enforce prohibition laws. Mississippi, which had made alcohol illegal in 1907, was the last state to repeal Prohibition in 1966. Interestingly enough, Moore County, where the Jack Daniel's distillery is located, is one of Tennessee's dry counties. Therefore, while it is legal to distill the product within the county, it is illegal to purchase it there.

- The original Volstead Act had defined "intoxicating beverage" as a product that had an alcohol content in excess of 0.5%. Non alcoholic beers (and wines) to this day have 0.5% Alcohol in the US as well as in Canada.

- At first, a beer with a maximum of 3.2% Alcohol By Weight (4% Alcohol By Volume), also referred to as "three-two beer" was allowed. Six months later, this restriction was lifted on a federal level, but Minnesota. Kansas, Oklahoma, Utah and Colorado to this day allow grocery stores to carry only "3.2" beer.

- Those involved in the alcohol business are still subjected to rigorous financial audits and checking of their criminal records - to deter the involvement of the organized crime in the alcohol business. In addition, the 3-tier alcohol distribution system was introduced throughout the US.

- The homebrewing boom was not sustained after Prohibition. The often muddy, unpalatable, and amateurish beers of the homebrewer lost favor to the beers produced by the professional brewers. Homebrewing did not become legal until 1979.

- On the eve of Prohibition in 1920, there were 1,400 Breweries across America. In 1935, two years after the end of prohibition, there were only 160 breweries. It would be another 75 years before America would have over 1,000 operating breweries, with all the new breweries being craft and micro breweries.

WHAT'S YOUR PLEASURE?

Pairing of our beers with cheese and other foods

Minhas Light

Minhas Light is an excellent light beer with plenty of flavor. It has only 97 calories and 3.6 gram of carbohydrates. It is made with 2-Row malted barley and domestic hops. The alcohol content is 4% by volume.

Cheese and Other Food Pairings: Mild semi-soft cheeses such as Havarti and Camembert; grilled fish, steamed vegetables.

Mountain Crest / Mountain Creek / Minhas Creek

These fine Canadian-style lagers are full-bodied and crisp, they start with a gentle maltiness and finish cleanly. They are made with 2-Row Canadian Malt and domestic hops. The alcohol content is 5.5% by volume.

Cheese and Food pairings: Sharp aged cheddar cheeses and aged smoked Gouda, thick-cut steaks and grilled vegetables as well as sharp aged cheeses.

Lazy Mutt Farmhouse Ale

Mutt is an unfiltered, light bodied ale with a malty nose and a slight citrus palate. A low alcohol presence allows more complex flavors to shine through. It is made with 2-Row malted barley, wheat malt, caramel and Vienna malts, and domestic hops. The alcohol content is 5% by volume.

Cheese and Food pairings: Swiss and Cheddar Cheese; crusty breads, fruit, and grilled meats.

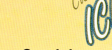

Clear Creek Ice

Clear Creek Ice is a classic Canadian Ice Lager. It starts with a gentle maltiness and finishes with a satisfying hop and a mild alcohol bite. It is made from Canadian 2-Row malted barley and domestic hops. The alcohol content is 6.2% by volume.

Cheese and Food Pairings: Well aged sharp cheeses such as Swiss and cheddar; roasted and BBQ meats.

1845 "All Malt" PILS

A truly classic European style pilsner beer, 1845 PILS starts out with light malt aromas followed by floral hop scents. A brilliant hop bitterness rolls lightly to the sides of the tongue, refreshed and cleansed with each sip. A perfect accompaniment to any meal, 1845 PILS matches even the most discriminating palate. The alcohol content is 5.5% by volume.

Cheese and Food Pairings: Gouda Cheese, spicy meat soups and stews, sautéed vegetables.

Swiss Amber Ale

At first glance, this reddish-copper Ale looks strong and heavy, but one sip proves that it is smooth as silk. Slight citrus notes greet you while aromatic hops tingle on your tongue. A smooth, clean finish waits at the bottom of the glass. Swiss Amber Ale is made with Brewer's 2-Row Malt, CaraPils Malt, Caramel Malts and domestic hops. The alcohol content is 5.5% by volume.

Cheese and Food Pairings: Romano and Parmesan Cheeses, hearty stews, roasted meats, fruit pastries.

Fighting Billy Bock Beer

Fighting Billy Bock Beer is a rich, flavorful, full-bodied beer reminiscent of traditional German bock beers of the past. As you lift the glass, malty sweet aromas fill your senses with a caramel sweetness. A gentle mix of floral scents greets the palate with a distinct yet delicate hop bitterness. Robust smoothness defines this classic beer. Fighting Billy Bock is made with Brewer's 2-Row Malt, CaraPils Malt, Caramel Malt, Black Malt and domestic hops. The alcohol content is 5.5 % by volume.

Cheese and Food pairings: Soft and semi-soft cheeses such as spiced Havarti and Limburger; vegetable soups, stews, heavier sauces and salty foods.

Rescue of Heritage Brands from Now Defunct Breweries

Over the years, the Brewery in Monroe has survived and prospered by rescuing brands and buying equipment from several breweries that were closing down. Two of these brands - Berghoff and Rhinelander - are still being produced by the Minhas Craft Brewery.

AUGSBURGER "the first Super-premium Craft Brewed" Beer Brand in America:

Augsburger beer made the Brewery in Monroe famous across the country. The Augsburger (nicknamed the "Augie") was the first super-premium craft brewed beer in the USA, although it did not get its start that way. In fact, it got its start in the underworld of the Chicago mafia.

The original "Augie" was brewed by the Monarch Brewery; one of the few successful breweries that Chicago has had in its history. In 1958, a former bootlegger took control of the brewery. During Prohibition (1920 to 1933), Al Capone had taught a lot of his associates the ins and outs of beer distribution.

A common sales technique used by the mafia at the time was a simple but effective one: a pipe bomb through the front window of neighborhood bars (then called saloons) whose owners tried to order beer from a rival bootlegger. Needless to say, beer sales soared with such imaginative marketing techniques.

In 1959, the Monarch Brewery launched Augsburger beer and gave the brew an air of respectability by labelling it as being brewed by "The House of Augsburg". When the brewery closed in 1967, the label was acquired by the Potosi Brewing Company located in the town of Potosi, Wisconsin (65 miles west of Monroe). The Potosi Brewery closed its doors in 1972.

Upon closure of the Potosi Brewery, the Augsburger brand was bought by Fred Huber (among other brands owned by Potosi). Fred Huber immediately converted the Augsburger beer into a "craft-brewed" beer. He was one of the most innovative brewery owners at the time. He tossed aside the old formula, and started brewing a richer tasting, maltier beer with a generous infusion of "noble" hops. It had more calories per bottle compared to other beers; but of course, the idea of being easy on your weight by drinking light beer was just taking shape. And Dr. Robert Atkins was 20 years away from inventing the "low carb diet". The new brew was developed and perfected under the expert hands of brewmasters Dave Radzanowski and Hans Kestler, the German trained brewmaster.

Dave Radzanowski was the brewmaster at the Monroe Brewery from 1973 to 92. He was instrumental in creating many recipes for the Brewery including Augsburger, Augsburger Dark and Augsburger Bock. He left the Brewery to become president of the famous Siebel Institute of Brewing Technology in Chicago.

The Augsburger in the unique green bottle was an instant hit. In 1973 when Augie was brought to the Monroe Brewery, it sold only 32,000 cases per year. This was increased to 2.5 million cases within the next 12 years, representing 60% of the total production of 250,000 barrels of the entire brewery.

Augie became very popular in Illinois, Wisconsin, Minnesota and other Midwest states. It was one of the best selling super-premium beers in the Midwest. Many people around the world claimed that Augie was the best beer they had tasted anywhere. Fred Huber, the owner and president of the Brewery even received the keys to the town of Augsburg, Germany for making it so famous across America. In 1978, the well respected *Great American Beer Book* published by Caroline House Publishers Inc. of Illinois listed Augie as the "best beer brewed in America".

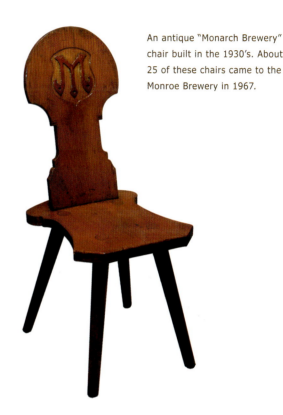

An antique "Monarch Brewery" chair built in the 1930's. About 25 of these chairs came to the Monroe Brewery in 1967.

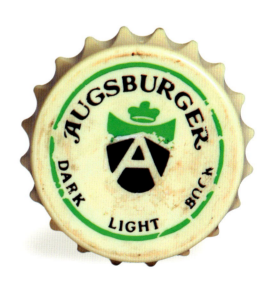

> One taste and you'll swear our Brewmaster was born in a Bavarian brewery.
>
> (Actually, he was. Really.)

This ad was referring to Hans Kestler.

The Augie was promoted by airing silly thirty-second radio spots starring the brewmaster, Hans Kestler, that caught the collective ears and wallets of beer drinkers. The image-spinners recruited him for a series of beer commercials and gained him fame as the voice of Augsburger. In fact, beermaking was in Kestler's blood. He was literally born in a brewery in the Bavarian region of Germany. For years, the heavily accented German brewer would tongue-in-cheek his way through a series of ads pitching his beer, sounding a bit like Arnold Schwarzenegger as a happy drunk. Also, the famous advertising line of "Hans made" was developed.

It is difficult to describe a radio commercial in a book, but it is perhaps best explained by a Letter to the Editor of a newspaper in Chicago by a reader who remembers the commercial:

"The cleverest advertising campaign I can recall for a beer was done on radio for Augsburger beer out of Monroe, Wisconsin, and involved interviews with a man purporting to be Hans Kestler, the resident Augsburger braumeister. I particularly recall one where he tried to reach the country-music audience by doing a German-accented square dance call that started, "Swing your partner and do-si-do; Augsburger beer is the best, you know," and then went on from there."

Fame did indeed have its price. Hans Kestler, brewmaster at Joseph Huber Brewing Company in Monroe, Wisconsin, had to get an unlisted telephone number because curious beer imbibers called his home at all hours to see if he was for real. The problem arose because Bavarian-born Kestler had a delightful accent that made him sound like a stage German.

In 1985, brewery owner Fred Huber sold the brewery to MTX Inc. of Milwaukee, owned by Bill Smith (former president of Pittsburgh Brewery and Pabst Brewing Company) and R. Craig Werle, (another former Pabst executive) for a reported sum of $7.8 million.

Pabst was the fourth largest brewery in America and one of the trio of brewing companies (Miller and Schlitz were the other companies) that earned Milwaukee the title of "Beer Capital of America" when it supplied one in four bottles of beer to Americans. The famous "Laverne and Shirley" sitcom was also based in a "make believe" Milwaukee brewery.

Hans Kestler was soon let go by Smith and Werle. This proved to be the beginning of the end of the Augsburger brand. In 1988, Smith and Werle sold the Augsburger Brand to Stroh Brewery of Detroit, Michigan, one of the largest mega breweries in America at the time. Stroh started making the Augie in Stroh's Minneapolis Brewery. Soon after, Stroh expanded Augsburger to 37 states with plans to distribute it nationally to compete with Budweiser, Coors and Miller beers. However, it was reported that Stroh never got the real Augsburger recipe.

The business situation at the Monroe Brewery got worse after its flagship brand was sold. Smith and Werle announced their intention to close the Brewery unless a suitable buyer was found. Fred Huber along with other investors bought back the brewery in 1989 for $2.25 million but were unable to get the Augsburger label back from Stroh.

The newspapers put out reports that the original Augsburger was made only with barley, hops, yeast and water - but now they also use corn and low quality hops". Stroh refused to comment. Whatever the reasons, with Stroh Brewery making the Augsburger, it lost its character and the beer drinkers noticed.

By the time Stroh sold its operation to Pabst in 1999 and divided its portfolio of various regional brands between Pabst and Miller in the buyout, the Augsburger label was as good as dead. Pabst stopped production of the once great tasting Augsburger beer in 2000 to concentrate on its core brands. After three years of unavailability, the Augie was produced by the Stevens Point Brewery under a license arrangement from the Pabst Brewery; however, its sales were a fraction of what they used to be at the peak of its popularity. The Stevens Point Brewery also stopped producing Augie in the fall of 2007.

> *There is one part of my job I hate. Contrary to what many think, there really is such a thing as bad beer. I know this because I have sampled a bunch of my competitors' beers. Ah but a damn good beer makes up for all the suffering.*
>
> *- Ravinder Minhas*

Berghoff

Berghoff Brewery, Fort Wayne, Indiana (1887 to 1990)

Berghoff is a full bodied European style premium beer brewed using the recipes Herman Berghoff (Sr.) brought with him from the Dortmund region of Germany in the 1870s. Herman Berghoff and his brother were headed west in 1870 to make their fortune, when their train stopped at Fort Wayne, Indiana (350 miles southeast of Monroe Wisconsin). Young Herman got off the train to buy a pretzel and someone offered him a job. He quickly went back into the train, grabbed his brother and accepted the job.

Over the next 17 years, Herman Berghoff and his 3 brothers acquired various businesses. In 1887, they raised $100,000 to start construction of Berghoff Brewery on Grant Avenue in Fort Wayne, Indiana. The building was almost complete when it was destroyed by a fire on August 22, 1887. Undaunted, the Berghoff brothers started to rebuild the Brewery on a more extensive scale. Newspapers reported that Herman was in his office writing telegrams seeking financial help from suppliers while the fire raged overhead. Another $140,000 was spent to rebuild the Brewery. The first year's output of the new Herman Berghoff Brewing Company was only 12,000 barrels of beer. Artificial refrigeration and bottling was installed in 1889. Brewery's production quickly rose to 90,000 barrels in 1890. The brewery filtered the water taken from a well 200 feet below the engine room. Berghoff Beer was introduced

at the Chicago's World Fair in 1893. To coincide with that event, Herman went to Chicago and opened the Berghoff Restaurant at State and Adams Streets in the heart of Chicago's Loop.

The Berghoff family was very successful and they were dedicated to the community that made it possible. Henry Berghoff was elected Mayor in 1902. He also founded the German-American National Bank. Gustav Berghoff formed the Rub-No-More Soap Company, which was purchased by Proctor & Gamble in 1925.

Public sentiment became increasingly anti-alcohol and anti-German on the eve of World War I. While the Berghoffs were proud of their German ancestry, they also loved the country that had given them success. When America entered the war against their homeland, Henry made a tearful announcement to his workers. He expressed loyalty to his adopted country and pledged his support in the war against Germany. He ordered that the American flag be flown above the plant and the company slogan be changed from "A Real German Brew" to "A Real Honest Brew".

With the onset of Prohibition, the industrious family remained positive about the future. The brewery became the Berghoff Products Company during the dry years and promoted "Bergo", a soft drink, and Berghoff Malt Tonic. Company advertising hailed their malt tonic as "recommended by the medical professional for nursing mothers, convalescents, the undernourished, tired, and rundown." It was also said to aid digestion and be healthful for young and old alike."

When the Volstead Act was repealed in 1933, the Berghoff Brewery was ready. It was the first Indiana brewer to produce legal three - two beer (3.2% Alcohol By Weight).

Brewing Up A Damn Good Story

A new generation of Berghoff sons had come of age during the dry years. They wanted to follow in the footsteps of their fathers. Gustav Berghoff's sons opened the Hoff-Brau Brewing Company in the empty Rub-No-More Soap building in 1934. Hoff-Brau was noted for its pioneer advertising and quality beers: Hoff Brau Bock, Golden Ale, Gold Star, and Dry Pilsner. Their ads were heavy on sports and nostalgia, and promoted safe driving. Hoff Brau was described as "the beer without a headache", and a 1934 booklet advised parents that "growing children need a small glass with every meal".

By 1950, sales at both Berghoff-owned breweries were flat and both plants were in need of modernization. Updating equipment and competing in the new mass market arena with national brands wasn't financially possible for the family-owned businesses. The Hoff-Brau Brewing Company closed its doors in 1951. A block away, the Berghoff Brewery was sold in 1954 to the much larger Falstaff Brewing Corporation of St. Louis, the second largest brewing company in the country at the time. However, the Berghoff family retained the rights to the Berghoff brands, labels and the recipes.

Falstaff Brewing Corporation was later purchased by Paul Kalmanovitz, head of S&P Corporation and its General Brewing Company, which is now Pabst Brewery. The original Berghoff Brewery was eventually shut down in 1990. S&P did receive an offer from Labatt's of Canada to produce its beers in Fort Wayne, but the offer was rejected. Instead, 95 percent of the brewery equipment was shipped to China for a new Pabst Brewery in the People's Republic. In the fall of 1992, the wrecking ball reduced a century of brewing history to rubble. Two warehouses used for storage are all that remain at the brewery site.

Berghoff Restaurant, Chicago, IL (Established 1898)

The Berghoff Restaurant, at 17 West Adams Street, near the center of the Chicago Loop, was opened in 1898 by Herman Joseph Berghoff and has become a Chicago landmark. He sold Berghoff beer made in the Berghoff Brewery in Fort Wayne Indiana for a nickel, and the sandwiches were offered for free. The bar remained open even though it was one of the few bars that did not turn into a speakeasy; instead during Prohibition, it sold the legal "near beer" and Bergo soda pop and became a full service restaurant. After Prohibition was repealed in 1933, the Berghoff was issued Liquor License No. 1. To this day, this license number is displayed in the restaurant's window with pride.

For all his great qualities, Herman Berghoff was an old fashioned man. In fact, he lifted a mug at his Berghoff Restaurant in Chicago in 1933 and declared, "Ladies will not be seated at the bar. We can't handle them when they drink strong liquor". Berghoff maintained a separate men's only bar for many decades. The segregation ended in 1969, when seven members of the National Organization for Women sat at the bar and the very famous Gloria Steinem demanded the much publicized drink.

The Berghoff family still runs a restaurant at the same location in Chicago. They also have a Berghoff Café at the Chicago's O'Hare International Airport Terminal 1 (United Airlines). The Berghoff Restaurant and Café has served Berghoff beers for 110 years. Minhas Craft Brewery proudly brews all the Berghoff beers in cans, bottles and Kegs, which are sold in the Berghoff restaurants as well as hundreds of other bars and retailers in Chicago, the rest of Illinois and other states in the Midwest. The equivalent of 400,000 cases of Berghoff Beers are produced annually at the Minhas Craft Brewery.

The Berghoff Restaurant in the heart of Chicago Loop.

The Potosi Brewery

The town of Potosi, Wisconsin is located on the Mississippi River and in the tri-state area of Wisconsin, Illinois and Iowa. It is 65 miles west of Monroe Wisconsin. The Potosi Brewing Company opened in 1852. Potosi was purchased by the Schumacher brothers in 1886 and the brewery remained in family hands until it closed on December 31, 1972, suffering from a lack of family members to carry on the business. The Brewery reached a peak of 75,000 barrels in annual production in its 120 year history. Joseph Huber bought the Augsburger, Bohemian Club, Potosi, Holiday and Alpine, Barrel of Beer and Our Beer brands upon its closure.

The historical Potosi Brewery building has now been converted into the National Brewery Museum by the American Breweriana Association at a cost of $5 million. It attracts tens of thousands of visitors from the tri-state area and the rest of the country.

Potosi beer was produced at the Potosi Brewery from 1933 to 1972. Potosi beer was produced and marketed in Monroe from 1973 to 1988. We still produce this beer on contract on occasion in small quantities.

The well travelled Bohemian Club beer got its start at the Joliet Citizen Brewery (Joliet, IL) in 1945. Its production was moved to the Monarch Brewery (Chicago, IL) from 1958 to 1967, moving to Oconto Brewery (Oconto, WI) till 1968. It then came to Potosi Brewery (Potosi, WI) from 1968 to 1972 until its closure. The Monroe Brewery produced Bohemian Club Beer from 1972 to the early 1980's.

The Holiday beer was introduced by Potosi in 1956. Holiday Beer sold extremely well in Chicago and Milwaukee. The Brewery even did private brands for the Armanetti's Liquor Store chain in Chicago and the Kellers Liquor Store chain in Milwaukee. It is interesting to note that Mr. Kellers was part of the famous Schlitz Beer family from Milwaukee. Upon closure of the Brewery in 1972, the Monroe brewery purchased the brand and produced it from 1973 till 1978.

Alpine beer was produced at Potosi from 1963 to 1972. Upon its closure, The Monroe Brewery produced it from 1973 to 1977

This unique style of glass bottle was brewed and packaged at the Monroe Brewery from 1973 to 1980. It is interesting to note that this bottle shape concept is very similar to the green Mickey's beer bottle - although it appears there is no connection between the two brands or breweries.

Brewing Up A Damn Good Story

Rhinelander Brewery

Rhinelander Brewery was established in 1893. It was located 250 miles straight north of Monroe Wisconsin, in the northwoods country of northern Wisconsin. With the exception of the Prohibition years, it produced the Rhinelander beer and Rhinelander bock until 1967 when the brewery was shut down permanently. Rhinelander beer has since been produced at the Brewery in Monroe.

In 1940, the Rhinelander Brewery came out with little 7 oz. (207 mL) bottles with painted labels and called them Rhinelander "shorties". The shorties were a great success and the Monroe Brewery produced the Rhinelander Shorties for many years. Many other breweries followed by producing their product in the same package. Ironically, Corona has recently introduced its beer in a 7 oz. bottle size (called Coronitas) and is having great success - proving that consumers still like the idea of the "shorties".

The 70's "Shorties".

Peter Hand Brewery

Established in 1891 and located at 1000 West North Avenue in Chicago, the Peter Hand Brewery has had a long time connection with the Monroe Brewery. The Peter Hand Brewery was closed during Prohibition from 1920 to 1933 but re-opened in 1933. It became very successful in the 1960s when it sold over 1 million barrels of beer - mostly for its flagship brand Meister Brau - and had revenues in excess of $50 million. In 1967 it changed its name to Meister Brau Brewing Company. It fell into tough financial times and sold the Meister Brau brand to Miller Brewing Company of Milwaukee in the late 1960s. The Meister Brau Brewing Company went bankrupt in 1972.

In 1973, Fred Huber, son of the Joseph Huber of the Joseph Huber Brewing Company in Monroe, Wisconsin, along with other investors, purchased the Meister Brau Brewery with its 17 buildings along with the Old Chicago, Spartan, Extra Pale and Zodiac brands for $1.35 million. They resurrected the brewery under its original name - Peter Hand Brewery, sold a lot of beer under its new flagship brand Old Chicago from 1973, but finally closed it in 1978. Fred Huber was president of Peter Hand Brewery from 1973 to 1978 and at the same time, he was the vice president of Joseph Huber Brewing Company in Monroe, Wisconsin. When the Peter Hand Brewery was closed, a lot of its equipment including ageing and fermentation tanks were brought to the Brewery in Monroe. Also, a few brands, including Old Chicago, Van Merritt and Braumeister - were bought and produced at the Monroe Brewery for many years to come.

Ironically, in the entire history of Chicago, there have been very few breweries in the city despite its large population, and the breweries that have been in Chicago, they have been very small. Throughout the city's history, most of the beer sold in Chicago has come from Wisconsin and other states.

The Story of Light Beers

The Peter Hand Brewery and Fred Huber also had a connection with the introduction of light beer in the USA and the rest of the world.

Light beer was invented by the biochemist, brewmaster and inventor of Ukrainian origin Dr. Joseph L. Owades at New York's Rheingold Brewery when he introduced the "Gablinger's Diet Beer" in 1967. Dr. Owades came to be regarded as the father of light beer. While working in Brooklyn, N.Y., at Rheingold Breweries, he developed a process to remove the starch from beer. This reduced its carbohydrates and calories.

Light Beer advertising in its infancy.

As Dr. Owades explained, "When I got into the beer business, I used to ask people why they did not drink beer," "The answer I got was two fold: One, 'I don't like the way beer tastes.' Two, 'I'm afraid it will make me fat.' "It was a common belief then that drinking beer made you fat,". "I couldn't do anything about them not liking the taste of beer, but I could do something about the calories."

The Gablinger's Diet Beer had a television advertisement showing a man with the girth of a sumo wrestler shovelling spaghetti into his mouth and downing a Gablinger's Diet Beer. It did not succeed and a few years later, Dr. Owades left the brewery and started consulting for other Breweries. He consulted with the Chicago Brewery and gave them the light beer recipe. They did a line extension of their flagship brand Meister Brau and called it "Meister Brau Lite". As Mr. Owades routinely joked, "Being from Chicago, they couldn't spell 'light'."

Upon acquisition, Miller reformulated the recipe and re-launched the Meister Brau as "Lite Beer from Miller" in 1975. Miller heavily marketed the Miller Lite using the slogan 'tastes great, less filling' and used masculine pro-sports players and other macho figures of the day in an effort to sell to the key beer-drinking male demographic. Miller's approach worked and soon Miller Lite became its number one brand. Of course, other breweries also introduced light beers including the Anheuser-Busch Brewery. In fact, Bud Light is currently the largest selling brand in the USA.

Huber re-introduced Old Chicago in Chicago and also exported it to Britain, Paraguay and Argentina.

Van Merritt Brand

The Van Merritt beer brand was launched at the Burlington Brewing Company in Burlington, Wisconsin in 1934, right after the end of Prohibition. Van Merritt beer was produced there for 21 years and then it went to the Joliet Citizen Brewing Company (Joliet, Illinois) from 1955 - 58, Monarch Brewing Company (Chicago, Illinois) from 1958 - 66, Oconto Brewing Company (Oconto, Wisconsin) from 1966-68, Potosi Brewery (Potosi, Wisconsin) from 1968-72. In 1973, Fred Huber tried to rescue the Chicago's Peter Hand Brewery by introducing a crisply hoppier version of Van Merritt Beer when the Potosi Brewery shut down. This did not work as Chicagoans remained stubbornly loyal to Heileman's Old Style from LaCrosse, Wisconsin for many more years. When the Peter Hand Brewery finally closed in 1978, Van Merritt beer's production was moved to the Monroe Brewery. This continued until 1985 when its production was finally ceased.

Braumeister

Sold under the slogan "Milwaukee's Choicest", Braumeister Beer got its start at the Independent Brewery in Milwaukee Wisconsin in 1901. It was produced at that brewery until it was shut down in 1964. G. Heileman Brewery then bought the brand and produced it in their breweries in Newport (Kentucky), Sheboygan (Wisconsin) and LaCrosse (Wisconsin) until 1970, at which time the Monroe Brewery bought the brand and started producing it. Braumeister Beer was produced there until 1975 when its production was shifted to the Peter Hand Brewery in Chicago, Illinois, run by Fred Huber. When the Chicago Brewery was closed in 1978, the production of the Braumeister brand came back to Monroe, but was discontinued shortly thereafter.

In its 51 years of history, and with its slogan "The World's Most Honored Beer", Van Merritt Beer might not have been the "most honored", but it would be among the "world's most travelled beers".

> *Beer represents life in its entirety - water, good smell, great flavor, happiness, grain, energy and froth. Did I mention hoppiness?*
>
> *- Manjit Minhas*

Ad Persuasion

Most TV advertisements for the beer feature a few beautiful women with a beer-swilling "male fool". The "male fool" ditches the woman for the cold beer. Presto! Instant (and yawningly typical) comes out the beer marketing campaign. A variation is where the "male fool" gets the beautiful women when he has the beer. While there is nothing wrong with this genre of beer advertising, the Brewery in Monroe and its owners have been associated with a number of beer advertising innovations. In fact, many of them were ahead of their time. Some of the examples are given in this chapter:

Television Ads

One of the major reasons that our brews are very popular in Alberta and Manitoba in Canada are our unique television ads. We have produced about 20 TV commercials to date. The creative concepts for almost all our commercials are generated in-house and are usually produced in Los Angeles and Calgary. The ads are frequently based on personality profiles, poking fun at ourselves and the competition, and occasionally include pretty girls and automobiles. In 2008, we used an animated ad for marketing the Lazy Mutt Farmhouse Ale in Wisconsin with much success. We had fun with a very active dog representing the mutt and his two friends chasing and "cow tipping" a spotted cow. Spotted Cow happens to be a successful craft brew produced in New Glarus, 10 miles north of Monroe, Wisconsin.

Most of our TV ads can be seen on the internet (www.YouTube.com and our website www.MinhasBrewery.com).

Cans Versus Bottles

The can versus bottle TV ad which aired from 2004 to 2007 in the Manitoba (Canada) market created a revolution in the marketplace. In this advertisement, Manjit Minhas compared the virtues of drinking beer out of a can versus drinking out of a bottle for the Minhas Creek Classic Lager brand. In this ad, she talked about how the cans are 100% recyclable versus all the water and chemicals that have to be used to clean the returnable bottles.

Russian made Camera used by Moni Minhas from 1967 to 1976 in New Delhi, India. Perhaps Moni's children - Ravinder and Manjit Minhas got their video talent from this experience for making successful TV Ads!

Of course, Ms. Minhas also explained in the TV ad the fact that returnable bottles are often used for ashtrays by the consumers before returning them. Success of this TV ad campaign is indicated by the fact that 75% of beer sold in Manitoba today is packaged in cans. The canned beer market was only 30% prior to this advertising campaign.

Radio Ads

Mountain Crest Classic Lager, one of our major brands in Alberta, (Canada) was the official "3 Star Selection" sponsor for the National Hockey League's (NHL's) Calgary Flames Team during 2003-2004 season on its official radio broadcast. We are happy to report that the Calgary Flames Team went all the way to the Stanley Cup Finals in that year.

Recently, we have had radio ads for iEnergy on the National Basketball Association's (NBA) Milwaukee Bucks team radio network across Wisconsin.

Our brewery has had some of the most innovative and successful beer ads on radio in Wisconsin and Chicago. There are many people who can still repeat verbatim some of the Augsburger ads done by the brewmaster Hans Kestler with his delightful German accent in the late 1970s and 1980s. With his German accent dripping from each word like foam down the side of a freshly filled stein, Hans would extol the virtues of Augsburger and Berghoff beers with a quaintness that bordered on the satiric. Also, there were the Berghoff ads by Fred Huber, the then owner of the Brewery and Herman Berghoff, owner of the famous Chicago restaurant.

Of course, it is very difficult to impart the flavor of these ads in a book; however, scripts for some of the memorable radio ads are given below. The reader can also visit our Visitor Center at the Brewery in Monroe to listen to about 10 of the radio ads. Of course, you would also want to take the "Best Brewery Tour in America".

The antique Minhas Family "Murphy" radio circa 1940s, brought from India.

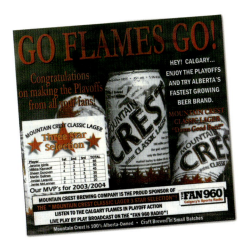

Mountain Crest advertising the results of its "3 Star Selection" after each Calgary Flames Hockey Game.

Here are some texts:

Talking Sharpie from Hollywood Ad - Hans Kestler, brewmaster for Augsburger

Many people question whether I'm the real Augsburger brewmaster or just some mouth talking sharpie from Hollywood. One sip of our Augsburger should make it perfectly clear: Could an actor brew beer this flavorful? No way Jose! Augsburger has won blind taste tests in cities all over America and it is ranked #1 in *"The Great American Beer Book."* You don't get that from hanging out on the corner of Sunset and Vine. It takes an authentic brewmaster to give Augsburger its quality. So Bunky, if you figure I was just some slick dude from Tinseltown, forget that noise.

Bar and Grille Ad - Hans Kestler, brewmaster for Augsburger

Because Augsburger is an authentic American beer, where better to enjoy it than here, an authentic American Bar and Grille. "Hey Hans, tell that cook back there that I'm real hungry." You got it. Hey Chow Runner, I've got a real Bean Buster up here. "Uh, let me have a ham sandwich on a roll." Ordering a pie on a pillow. "Add an onion." Pin a rose on it. "Tell him no toothpicks." Hold the lumber. "And pour me an Augsburger, please." One brewski, an Augsburger. Augsburger is ranked #1 in the "Connoisseur's Guide to Beer" so naturally it's popular with the connoisseurs here. "Hey Hans, I'll have a brat and an Augsburger." Ordering an Augie and a doggie!

Berghoff and Blues:

Hello, my name is Hans Kestler, brewmaster at Huber Brewing Company, Monroe, Wisconsin. Do you like great music, do you like great beer? Then I have just the ticket for you a ticket to Berghoff and Blues Fest, Saturday, September 18, Green County, Fairgrounds in Monroe. Mark your calendar now and come on out and relax, listen to 9 great Blues Bands and enjoy cold Berghoff Beer, September, 19th, Monroe, cold Berghoff Beer, Hot Blues and good fun.

Our Production Manager Dick Tschanz is one of the main volunteers of the Berghoff and Blues Festival, raising funds for community projects.

Print Ads

Dry Beer

Asahi of Japan, after many years of research, started the "dry beer" trend in the 1980s, which then swept the North American markets. Molson introduced its "Special Dry" beer in Canada in 1989, followed by introduction of "Bud Dry" in 1990 in the USA and many other dry beers such as Rainier Dry and Olympia Dry. It is interesting that "Golden Glow" which was produced from the early 1900s to the 1950s, was advertising "dry" beer in the mid 1940s - about 40 years ahead of its time.

Light Beer – Non Fattening

Light beers are the number 1 selling beers in the US and they are growing at 10% per year in Canada. In the 1970s, Miller Lite became the first light beer in the US to be a major light brand, with the famous ad campaign "Tastes great, less filling".

Our brewery had a similar message, decades before the popularity of light beers, as evidenced by the adjacent ad.

"Double Dry Beer" ad Circa 1940s.

"Light Beer" ad Circa 1950s.

Right On Time

"Miller Time" and "If you've got the time, we've got the beer" advertising campaigns were used by Miller in the mid 1970s with great success.

Our brewery had a similar "RIGHT ON TIME" themed print advertising much earlier – in the 1950s.

Wanted Beer Distributors

Volkswagen's "Drivers Wanted" campaign, which was first launched in July 1995, has been widely recognized as a new approach to marketing. This fabulously successful marketing concept is credited with reviving Volkswagen sales in North America and is used in teaching marketing classes and seminars as a "case study" of a successful ad campaign.

Interestingly, a very similar advertising idea was used by the Huber Brewery in the 1950s.

"Right on Time" ad Circa 1940s.

Huber Brewery ad Circa 1950.

Sports Team Sponsorships

Our brewery sponsors many teams across Canada and the USA. Here are pictures of the Huber team uniforms used years ago. Interestingly, when Milwaukee got its major league baseball team, it was also named the "Brewers". We have also been official sponsors of the National Basketball Association's (NBA's) Milwaukee Bucks Team.

Mountain Crest Classic Lager has been the Official Sponsor of the Calgary Roughnecks, the professional lacrosse team as well as Alberta's MFC (Maximum Fighting Championship).

Attack Ads

We often say "If our competition likes us, we are not doing our job". In Canada, Molson and Labatt, our arch rival competitors, have attacked our brands by running ads reminding consumers that our brewery is located in the USA and not in Canada. This is a good indication that our competition is noticing us and that we are doing our job.

Much to our amusement, their ads have only helped us grow our brands.

Inclusion in Marketing Text Books

As mentioned earlier, we use aggressive and creative marketing techniques to promote our beers. This has been extensively written in the media as well as in Business School textbooks.

Two University text books on business & marketing have used the Minhas brother-sister duo in their "Case Studies".

96 | Ad Persuasion

Swag and More Swag

We routinely give away free branded stuff to our most loyal customers such as T shirts, golf shirts, beanie hats (called toques in Canada), poker chips, playing cards, beer glasses, neon signs and a variety of other stuff. These items help increase sampling of our Damn Good Beers and develop our brands.

> *In 1809, U.S. President James Madison appointed a "Secretary of Beer" to his cabinet.*

Public Relations

We believe that building good public relations is very important to the success of our business. It also happens that ours is a great story that the media loves to write about. Our public relations effort consists of being involved in the communities we sell our beers, attending and sponsoring political functions as well as having a visitor center, museum, and gift shop. Of course, having paid advertising is not the same thing as having articles and news stories written about us. In fact, we believe that the public relations success we have is priceless. Stories about our brewery and its brands appear in newspapers, television, magazines and on radio on a weekly basis.

"Best Brewery Tour in America"

Minhas Craft Brewery has a Visitor Center consisting of a museum, a gift store and the Lazy Mutt Lounge. It attracts thousands of visitors to the southern Wisconsin area.

The Museum has artifacts, cans, bottles, bottle labels, packaging boxes, malt records, accounting journals, neon signs, brewery sports team uniforms, pictures, company stock certificates, branded glassware and thousand of other items - going back to the early 1900s. We acquire artifacts for the museum on a continual basis. Many people from across the country have also donated historically relevant items to our museum. The gift store sells branded products such as golf shirts, T shirts, toques, beanie hats, poker chips, playing cards, neon signs and glassware.

The Lazy Mutt Lounge is where people taking the tours get to taste the freshest beers anywhere. They can also savor our old fashioned sodas and energy drinks. Our expert tour guides give explanation of various brews the visitors are tasting. Of course, they get to see our Brewhouse and other facilities and learn about our damn good beer making process. People taking the tour also get an 8 pack of samples of our beers and other products as a parting gift.

The Visitor Center is open Monday to Saturday and daily guided tours are offered. We also welcome large groups. Prior notification is recommended to enable us to offer prompt service. The telephone number at the Center is 1-800-BEER-205 (1-800-233-7205).

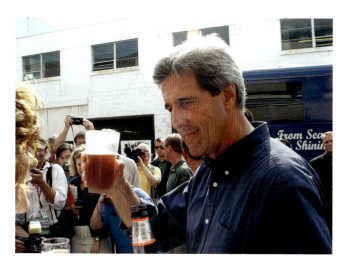

John Kerry's Visit:

In 2004, John Kerry, the US Presidential candidate for the Democratic Party and his election machine visited the Brewery. The Brewery was chosen as a way of showcasing what a progressive mid-size company can do in the heartland of mid-America. Of course, it was a good photo-op for them. John Kerry enjoyed our Amber Ale and his wife Teresa Heinz Kerry enjoyed our Wit Ale.

Ribbon Cutting by US Senator Herb Kohl:

In 2007, US Senator Herb Kohl visited the Minhas Craft Brewery and did the ribbon cutting for the new Warehouse and Distribution Center and the MCB Guest House.

Other Awards and Recognitions:

Our brewery has been given a number of awards and recognitions over the years that acknowledge the leadership role we play in the economy of southern Wisconsin.

Left to right: Ronnie Marsh (Mayor of Monroe), Manjit Minhas, Gary Olson (President of Minhas Craft Brewery), Ravinder Minhas and US Senator Herb Kohl.

Brewing Up A Damn Good Story

PROUD TREE HUGGERS!

At Minhas Craft Brewery, we are proud tree huggers! Serious tree hugging takes some ingenuity, changing of a few old wasteful habits and investing some capital. Almost always, the benefits flow back immediately, the investment makes good business sense and it makes us feel very good. We believe that we are at the forefront of the environmental revolution in the brewing industry.

Rather than sitting back basking in the glory of what we have achieved already, we continue to push ourselves and explore opportunities to further reduce our carbon footprint. Our eventual aim is to become carbon neutral. And only then will we have met our Gold Standard of Environmental Friendliness. Here are a few examples:

Ban the Incandescent Bulb: In 2007, Minhas Craft Brewery banned incandescent bulbs from its premises. We removed 835 incandescent energy wasting bulbs and replaced them with energy efficient fluorescent bulbs. We recouped our investment in about one year.

Recycle Cardboard: We recycle 200,000 lbs of cardboard every year. We also came up with an innovative design where we pack 48 cans per tray instead of the customary 24 cans per tray. This uses 18% less cardboard. This might not sound like a big deal but we produce almost 1 million of these cardboard trays in a year, saving a lot of trees.

Recycle Cans: We recycle 1 million lbs of aluminum cans per year. Our customers also recycle more than 97% of the cans we produce. In fact, drinking beer in cans is the most environmentally friendly way to drink beer since an aluminum can is 100% recyclable.

Recycle Glass: We recycle 340,000 lbs of glass per year. Our customers also recycle an estimated 60% of the bottles we produce which amounts to over 1 million lbs of glass.

Feed Spent Malt to the Cows: After we have finished making our brews, we deliver over 6 million lbs of spent malt to local farmers to feed their dairy cows. The cows love the taste and nutrition they get from the spent malt. The 2-row malt we use not only produces cleaner tasting beer than 6-row, the cows also prefer spent malt from the 2 row. And when the cows are given less of the spent malt as feed, they protest by reducing their milk output!

Do Not Wrap the Cases with Plastic: Many companies stretch wrap each of the cases they package with a plastic film. The stretch wrapping machine uses a large amount of electricity and the wrap material adds to the already filled landfills. We refuse to use any plastic stretch wrapping material on our trays and cases; instead we use intelligent design and manufacturing techniques to protect our product.

Put Health Warning on Products Voluntarily: We are the first and the only beer or liquor company (so far!) in Canada to voluntarily put a Health Warning on each can and bottle we sell in Canada. An elected Canadian Member of Parliament Paul Szabo from Toronto has been trying to convince Health Canada to require Health Warning on all alcohol cans and bottles, for over a decade. However, M.P. Paul Szabo and other organizations who have been lobbying for these changes have been vehemently opposed by major Canadian beer, wine and spirits companies, citing among other reasons for their opposition that the cost of complying with such a requirement will cost them millions of dollars.

Frankly we fail to understand the reasons for this opposition. In fact, it cost us very little to voluntarily put Health Warning on our cans and bottles, as the change was phased-in as we ran out of stock on the packaging of our old inventory. Instead of waiting for a government bureaucracy to make up its mind, we decided to do the right thing on our own. The Government of Alberta's FASD (Fetal Alcohol Spectrum Disorders) honored us with their highest community service award recognizing our courageous decision.

Reduce Use of Electricity, Natural Gas and Water: In the last 6 years, our Brewery has reduced the usage of electricity by 83%, natural gas by 77% and water by 67% for each barrel of beer produced. We are determined to reduce usage of these non-renewable resources by another 20% over the next three years. We have achieved these goals by replacing old equipment, implementing better maintenance procedures, having longer production runs and generally reducing waste. Did you know that the ingredients used in making beer with malted barley like ours require 1/3 rd less water than the grapes need in making wine? Also, if the beer is made with rice instead of barley, it takes much more water. And did you know that our production of beer in its totality is almost "carbon neutral"?

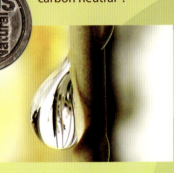

Support our Communities: We volunteer for various organizations and support charity golf tournaments including a tournament we hold in southern Alberta for the benefit of MADD (Mothers Against Drunk Driving). We formally mentor young people and middle managers in the community, and help out a number of university students with their projects and theses on subjects such as marketing, engineering and human resources.

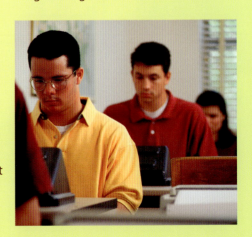

Sweet Libations and New Age Drinks

Our brewery was forced to go into non alcoholic beverages in 1920 at the onset of Prohibition. It entered this segment of the business in order to survive as a business; however, it turned out to be a blessing in disguise. Production at the Brewery actually increased as the Blumer's Golden Glow was extremely successful. With the introduction and success of Blumer's Old Fashioned Sodas, the iEnergy Energy Drink, Peelers and Corsairs Flavored Malt Beverages (FMBs), we expect this to continue to be an important segment of our business.

Blumers Old Fashioned Sodas

Our brewery, like many other craft breweries, produces old fashioned sodas. The Blumers Old Fashioned Sodas are sold in the Midwest with great success in six flavors - Root Beer, Orange Cream, Cream Soda, Black Cheery, Blueberry and Diet Root Beer.

> *Hey Dad - Give me a woman who loves beer as much as I do, and I will give you the 11 grandchildren you desperately want.*
>
> *- Ravinder Minhas*

Flavored Malt Beverages (FMBs):

In 1985, our Brewery became one of the first (if not the very first!) to produce FMBs in the USA when it started producing Savannah Coolers in three flavors – Alcoholic Lemonade, Raspberry and Fuzzy Navel. These were made with the lightest beer the Brewery had in its cellars. These were followed a few years later with our brewery producing Hoopers Hooch Coolers. The Brewery was about 15 years ahead of its time when the malt based cooler category became big with the introduction of Mike's Hard Lemonade, Smirnoff Ice and other such brands. It should be noted that at that time, the technology to produce FMBs was in its infancy. For the Minhas Craft Brewery to have the cutting edge technology to produce world class "malternatives", it would be another 20 years when our brewery purchased a Clear Malt System from Europe in 2008. The Brewery now produces the Corsairs and Peelers Mojito, Alcoholic Lemonade and Orange Squeeze.

We are also producing "Ready To Drink" Marco Polo Cordials, Spiced Rum and Coke, Coconut Rum, alcoholic energy drink and many other products - all made with the cleanest Clear Malt in the world.

iEnergy

Ravinder and Manjit Minhas introduced their energy drink under the brand name "iEnergy" in 2007. Red Bull and many other brands are growing at 40% per year and the energy beverage is now a multi billion dollar business.

Storing & Pouring Your Beer

Beer, like any other perishable food, needs the right care to make sure it tastes best when it is consumed. Here are a few practical tips:

Storing Beer

- A beer's shelf life is about 12 months. Heat and light are the worst enemies of beer.
- Store beer in a cool, dark place with a temperature of approximately 55 Degree Fahrenheit (12 Degree Celcius) or in a bar fridge set at 38 Degree Fahrenheit (3 Degree Celcius).
- Draft beer has to be refrigerated at all times.
- With the latest technology, cans with a special lining maintain the freshness of beer the same as glass bottles.

Pouring Beer

1. Start with a clean glass, without a residue of detergent, which reduces head retention. Rinse the glass with cold water before pouring.

2. Hold the glass at an angle with your left hand and the beer with your right hand (vice versa if you are a southpaw) and slowly pour the beer into the glass. Make sure that the beer hits the middle of the inside of the glass; it should flow down the rest of the way, which will release carbonation and build a nice head.

3. When the glass is about half full, start to turn the glass into an upright position and continue filling the rest of the glass. Leave just enough space for the foam to rise to the lip of the glass.

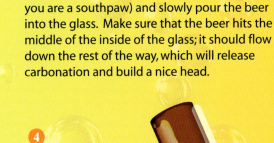

4. Do not dump the beer like you are filling your car's windshield washer, do not pour beer straight down the middle of the glass and do not slam the glass of beer on the table. These actions will create too much foam which makes beer drinking ungraceful and sloppy.

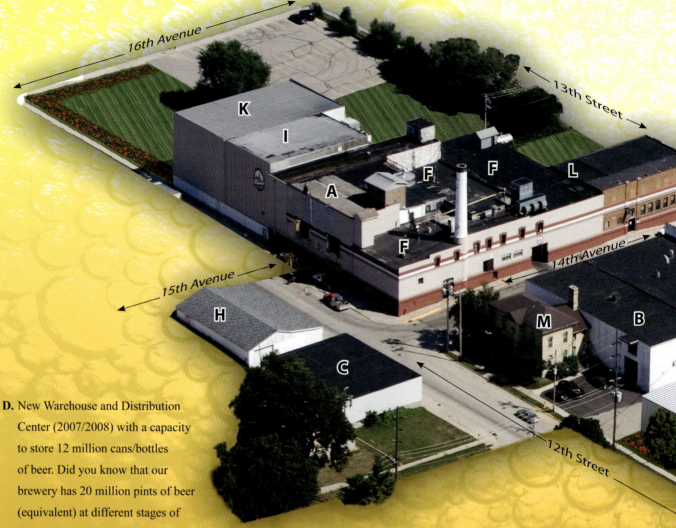

A. A, B and C Cellar Building (built 1934). The B Cellar (2nd floor) now has the state of the art technology Clear Malt System (2008). The C Cellar (main floor) now has the new Fermenters (2008).

B. Bottlehouse (1959) that has the packaging portion of the brewery. It houses the can and bottle fillers, the massive tunnel pasteurizer and remainder of the packaging lines.

It also has the other end of the "brewery tunnel" underneath the 14th avenue. Beer flows through the "Beer Tunnel" all day long, proving that "there is beer under the streets of Monroe".

C. Crown Shed (1966) now used for maintenance and parts storage.

D. New Warehouse and Distribution Center (2007/2008) with a capacity to store 12 million cans/bottles of beer. Did you know that our brewery has 20 million pints of beer (equivalent) at different stages of finish, at all times?

E. Old Warehouse (1971) that now houses the new Mead and Riverwood Twin Packing machines (2008), the automatic palletizers (2007) and some packaged goods.

F. Brewhouse, the oldest portion of the Brewery (1875, 1890 and 1900). This is where the magic of brewing occurs. It has the Brewkettle, the Mash/Lauter Tun and other brewing equipment.

G. Minhas Craft Brewery Guest House (2007), a 1,600 sq. ft. feet bungalow style house with double garage that is reserved for stay by our distributors, customers, guests, consultants and suppliers when they are visiting Monroe.

H. Hawaiian Shed (1952) that stores bagged malt and empty Kegs.

I. H, I and J Cellars (1970) that house the fermentation and ageing tanks.

J. Juice Garage (1976) that is used for storing packaging materials.

K. K Cellars Building (3 story) that houses ageing tanks (1978).

L. Office and MCB Visitor Center Building (1934). It also has the Lazy Mutt Lounge, Museum and Gift Center (2006).

M. Jailhouse Tap Bar that is now owned by a Monroe Family.

300 000 SQ. FT. OF HERITAGE BUILDINGS SPREAD OVER 7 ACRES OF LAND IN THE HEARTLAND OF AMERICA

Index

1845 " all malt" PILS.................28, 77
18th Constitutional Amendment ..10
3.2 Beer....................................73, 76
Advertising Strategies..................92
Ageing Cellars 41
Alamo Tequila..............................51
Alberta Centennial Medallion
Award...53
Alberta Venture Magazine 53
Alp & Dell....................................17
Amber Ale....................................26
Amcore Bank 59
American Breweriana
Association.................................86
America's Dairyland 10
Andechs Beer.........................49, 65
Anheuser-Busch...........................71
Asahi of Japan..............................95
Associated Press..........................48
Atlantic City.................................70
Augsburger............................49, 63-66,
....78-81
Awards Won.................................53
Badger Trail 16
Barrel of Beer...............................87
Baumgartner's.................10, 18, 19
Bavaria 32
Beck's..29
Belgium..................................23, 24
Benedictine Monks 49, 65
Berghoff.........................49, 63, 64, 66,
....82-85, 94
Berghoff Family 48
Best American made bock beer....34
Best Brewery Tour in America.....17, 98
Beverage Testing Institute............39
Bevo...71
Big Rock Brewery........................24
Bissinger 10, 48, 55
Blarney's Irish Cream 51
Blumer Brewery.............10, 48, 58, 59,
....70
Blumer's Old Fashioned Sodas....101
Blumer, Adam Jr. 58
Blumer, Adam Sr. 48
Blumer, Fred J............48, 58, 59, 73
Blumer, Jacob C..........................58
Blumer's Ice Cream 71
Bock Beer...............................32-35
Braumeister Beer 91
Brennan's.....................................17
Brew Kettle............................23, 40
Brown Swiss Cows 11
Budvar..29
Buildings Aerial Photo................104
Calgary, Alberta, Canada 47
Calgary Flames............................93
Calgary Inc. Magazine 53
Canadian Business Magazine 53
Canning, Bottling and Kegging ...41
Cantons of Switzerland 17
Capone, Al.............................70, 78
Cheese Days.............13, 20, 21, 27
Cheese Making Center 17

Cheesemakers 17
Chicago, IL...................................11
Chicago World Fair......................83
Chocolate Flavors 33
City Brewery, LaCrosse WI..47
Clear Creek Ice 77
Confucius 9
Connoisseur's Guide to Beer 39
Community Support...................100
Coors Brewery 36
Cork Dork 5
Corona...88
Corsairs FMBs 101
Courthouse 10
Cow Tipping.................................92
Crappo...71
Curse of the Billy Goat 33
Dark Lager 5
DE Filter.......................................41
Dempsey's Irish Ale.....................65
Devon Energy 51
Ditka, Mike 62
Dry Beer.......................................95
Duff Wine.......................................5
Einbeck Distributing Plant...........75
Eisenhower Agency, Freeport IL..75
Energy Conservation.................100
Environmental Stewardship.........22, 100
Esser, George........................48, 55
Falstaff Brewery..........................84
Family-owned Companies 44
Famo..71
Farmhouse Ale 23-25
Fermentation Tanks.....................40
Fetal Alcohol Spectrum Disorders
(FASD).......................................53
Fighting Billy Bock.............32-34, 77
First Bank of Monroe...................59
Flanders Region 23
Founder's Tap Room...................49
Freeport, Illinois...........................16
Gift Shop......................................49
Golden Glow Beer 48
Government Cellars 41
Graduate of the Last Decade
Award..53
Great American Beer Book 39, 79
Green County Courthouse...........13
Grist Mill......................................40
Health Warning............................52
Heaven Hill Distillery....................51
Hefty, Jacob................11, 48, 56
Heileman Brewery.......................65
Heineken......................................29
Hermann, John................48, 55, 56
Holiday Beer................................87
Homer Simpson............................5
Honeymoon, Origin of.................45
Hops..30
Huber...11
Huber Bock..................................61
Huber, Fred 48, 60-66, 79,
....89
Huber, Joseph........................48, 61

Husky Energy..............................51
Ice Lager 5
iEnergy......................................101
Illinois..47
In Flanders Field 24
Indiana...82
International Brotherhood
of Teamsters 49
J.I. Case Threshing Company 10
Jack Daniels Distillery 76
Jackson, Michael...................64, 65
Jailhouse Tap...............................14
Japan 43
John McCrae 24
Joliet Citizen Brewery, IL 91
Josef Groll...................................29
Kerry, John.............................49, 99
Kestler, Hans..........49, 63, 79, 80,
....92
Knipschildt, John M..............48, 55
Kohl, US Senator Herb 99
Kalav, Kris...................................36
Labatt Brewery......................84, 96
Lazy Mutt Farmhouse Ale ..22-25, 77
Lenahan, Tim 36
Lent 32
Light Beer 49, 90
Limburger Cheese.......................17
Lost Coast Brewery, CA 37
Luncheon, Origin of.....................34
Lybrand, Jacob............................12
Macleans Magazine 53
Madison.......................................11
Mafia 70
Malt Syrup...................................71
Manitoba, Canada 52
Marathon Oil Company 51
Marilyn Monroe 10
Marty..11
Marty, Carl O. 11, 48, 59, 60
Marty, Robert F. 60
Mash/Lauter Tun.........................40
Meister Brau Brewery............49, 90
Miller Brewery..................49, 90, 95
Milwaukee..............................11, 91
Milwaukee Bucks...................94, 96
Minhas Creek Classic Lager 77, 92
Minhas Light...............................77
Minhas, Manjit..................4, 5 18, 22,
....36, 42, 47,
....51-53, 92-102
Minhas School of Beer
Business Success.................42-50
Minhas, Moni and Rani...............51
Minhas, Ravinder............4, 5, 22, 33,
....37, 42, 47,
....51-54, 102
Minnesota....................................47
Minnesota Brewery................47, 67
Molson...96
Monarch Brewery 78, 79, 91
Monroe Arts Center.....................17
Monroe Brewery 48
Monroe Clinic 15

Monroe Evening Times.............17, 32, 73-76
Mother Earth................................46
Mountain Creek Classic Lager.....77
Mountain Crest Classic Lager......47, 77, 93
Mountain Crest Spirits 47
MTX Inc..................................49, 66, 80
Mystic Juice 49
National Basketball Association ..96
National Brewery Museum..........86
National Hockey League.............92
National Post...............................53
National Register of Historic
Places..13
Near Beer...............................70, 71
New York Times...........................39
Northwoods Resort Industry........59
O' Hare Airport............................85
OK Liquor Stores.........................51
Oktoberfest..................................31
Oldest Brewery in the Midwest ...5
Olson, Gary.................................67
Owades, Dr..............................89-90
Pablo 71
Pabst Brewery 49, 80, 84
Pacific Northwest, USA 40
Paine..12
Pale Ale...5
Pepsi..67
Peter Hand Brewery.........62, 63, 89-91
Peters, Tyler................................37
Pick'n Save..................................17
Piggly Wiggly...............................17
Pilsen, Czechoslovakia 25, 28
Pilsner 5
Pilsner Urquell 29
Potosi Brewery..............49, 63, 79, 86
Pouring Beer..............................103
Preston, Steve.............................66
Print Ads......................................95
Prohibition...................10, 33, 48, 59,
....70-76, 79
Public Relations 97
Punjab, India...........................47, 51
Racine, Wisconsin.......................10
Radbuza River.............................28
Radio Ads....................................93
Radzanowski, Dave.....................79
Railroad Museum........................16
Rathskeller 14
Rattan, Jarvis..............................12
Real Beer.....................................73
Recycling...................................100
Regal Brau 48
Rheingold Brewery 89
Rhinelander Brewery..........48, 63, 88
Rice Krispies...............................29
Roosevelt, Franklin D. 72
Royko, Bob..................................66
Ruegger, Captain...................48, 56
Rule of Thumb, Origin of 38
Saaz Hops...................................29
Saisoners....................................23
Sake..29
Sam Adams 24

Sampler Pack	5
Savannah FMBs/Coolers	49, 66, 102
Saskatchewan, Canada	47
Shorty	88
Siebel Institute of Technology	36, 79
Sierra Nevada	24
Smith, William	49, 63, 66, 80
Sparging	40
Speakeasies	71
Specialty Malts	37
Steinem, Gloria	85
Stella Artois	29
Stephens Point Brewery	52
Storing Beer	103
Stroh Brewery	36, 49, 81
Sugar Mill Share Certificate	51
Swag	97
Swiss Amber Ale	26, 27, 77
Swiss Cheese Capital of the World	11
Swiss Cheese Corporation	60
Swiss Colony	11
Switzerland	10
Tommyknocker Brewery	36
Trader Joe's	107
Tree Hugger	100
Turner Hall	14
TV Commercials	92
Union Made Symbol	37
University of Calgary	51, 53
Van Merritt Beer	91
Vancouver Island B.C., Canada	47
Vivo	71
Volkswagen	95
Volstead Act	70, 76, 83
Wal-Mart	17
Waldorf of the Wilderness	59
Walgreen	17
Warehousing and Distribution Center	41
Weinstein-Minkoff Family	66, 67
Werle, Craig	63, 66, 80
Western Canada	40
Whirlpool	40
Wine Enthusiast	49
Wine Snob	5
Wisconsin Club	49
Women Entrepreneurs	53
World Beer Championship	34, 39, 49
World Beer Gold Medals	36
Worlds War I	24
Wort	40
Yankton, South Dakota	60
Youngest Brewery Owners	5

"Simpler Times Lager", a brand we especially produce for the Trader Joe's Grocery Chain.